D0097709

Praise for RADICAL MIDDLE

"A provocative contribution to the movement toward a Radical Middle. As a charter member of that movement, I welcome it."
—Charles Peters, Founding Editor,
Washington Monthly

"Mark Satin has written a stirring, thoughtful and deeply-felt manifesto for a fresh approach to public policy and public dialogue. If you're weary of the politics of hyper-polarization and with the discussion of issues being practiced as a form of extreme combat, visit *Radical Middle*. You may find it's where you belong."
—Walter Truett Anderson, President,
World Academy of Art and Science

"Tired of pointless politics? Here's a wake-up call that cuts through the tiresome rhetoric of right and left. With a voice that is as clear as a summer's day, a mind that is extraordinarily well-informed, and a quality of judgement that is nothing short of wise, Mark Satin calls us back to the commons where we belong."
—Jay Ogilvy, Cofounder of Global Business Network
and author of *Creating Better Futures*

"Mark Satin asks the right questions, and comes up with surprising answers. This book is thought provoking, lively, and sure to promote debate across the political spectrum."
—Alisa Gravitz, Executive Director,
Co-op America

"Don't look for political correctness or for scoring of political points on behalf of the left or right in Mark Satin's *Radical Middle*. Satin is relentless in his willingness to shock the reader and shake the status quo in search of what works. *Radical Middle* will get you thinking and get us closer to the world we want by shamelessly borrowing what Satin sees as the best from all sides."

—Sam Daley-Harris, Director,
Microcredit Summit Campaign

"This book is a worthwhile effort to bypass all the ideological shouting and come up with consensus public policy solutions that most Americans can support. There are proposals here to outrage Right and Left (respectively) – but also some around which sincere people of good faith who care about their country should pursue a consensus."

—John McClaughry, former Senior Policy Advisor, Reagan
White House, and President of Ethan Allen Institute

"This is an extraordinary book. It provides a roadmap for political transformation."

—John Marks, President,
Search for Common Ground

"Rising above hot-collar polemics… this book strives to elucidate some vital issues of the day in a visionary manner while anchoring itself in practical reality."

—Graham Molitor, Vice President, World Future Society,
and former Chief Lobbyist, General Mills, Inc.

"There is a clear hunger in this country for a new kind of politics. Satin's book gives us a map for how we might travel from the world of old-fashioned gridlock to the world of fresh thinking and new possibility."

—Chris Gates, President,
National Civic League

RADICAL MIDDLE

The Politics We Need Now

MARK SATIN

Westview
PRESS

A Member of the Perseus Books Group

Copyright © 2004 by Center for Visionary Law

Published in the United States of America by Westview Press, A Member of the Perseus Books Group, 5500 Central Avenue, Boulder, Colorado 80301–2877, and in the United Kingdom by Westview Press, 12 Hid's Copse Road, Cumnor Hill, Oxford OX2 9JJ.

Find us on the world wide web at www.westviewpress.com

Westview Press books are available at special discounts for bulk purchases in the United States by corporations, institutions, and other organizations. For more information, please contact the Special Markets Department at the Perseus Books Group, 11 Cambridge Center, Cambridge, MA 02142, or call (617) 252-5298, (800) 255-1514 or email special.markets@perseusbooks.com.

A Cataloging-in-Publication data record for this book is available from the Library of Congress.
ISBN 0-8133-4190-6

The paper used in this publication meets the requirements of the American National Standard for Permanence of Paper for Printed Library Materials Z39.48-1984.

Text design by *Reginald R. Thompson*

Set in 10.8 New Caledonia by the Perseus Books Group

10   9   8   7   6   5   4   3   2   1

*For my sister Diane, my true hero,
and my nephews Phillip and Chris:
may they inhabit a world even half so kind
as the one I wish for them here.*

CONTENTS

Preface: Ignore the Noise   ix

PART ONE:
THE EMERGING NEW POLITICS

1   A Creative and Practical Politics   3
2   The Caring Person   11
3   Journey to the Radical Middle   21

PART TWO:
MAXIMIZE CHOICES FOR EVERYONE

4   Universal, Preventive Health Care:
     Too Sensible?   35
5   Law Reform as if People Mattered   47
6   How to Stop Being Dependent on Oil   57

PART THREE:
GIVE EVERYONE A FAIR START

7   Great Teachers, Great Teachers,
     Great Teachers   69
8   Affirmative Action for the Truly
     Disadvantaged—of Every Race   81
9   Jobs for Everyone. A Financial
     Nest Egg for Everyone, Too   91

PART FOUR:
MAXIMIZE HUMAN POTENTIAL

10   Corporations We Can Be Proud Of   103
11   Long Live Biotech—
      with Adult Supervision   115
12   Bring Back the Draft,
      for Everyone This Time   125

PART FIVE:
HELP THE DEVELOPING WORLD

13   Globalization—With Savvy and Feeling   137
14   Humanitarian Military Intervention:
      No More Rwandas!   149
15   Tough on Terrorism—and Tough
      on the Causes of Terrorism   161

PART SIX:
BE A PLAYER, NOT A REBEL

16   You Can Have a Career
      and Be Political, Too   175
17   Join Groups That Matter, and
      Push Them to the Radical Middle   187
18   Do Some Political Spadework.
      Then Run for Office and Win   197

Acknowledgments: Down at the Piccadilly   207
Index   211

PREFACE:
IGNORE THE NOISE

URN OFF *THE O'REILLY FACTOR*. Take Al Franken's book *Lies and the Lying Liars Who Tell Them* back to the bookstore. It can be satisfying to think of our political opponents as unprincipled and corrupt, and a threat to democracy and decency, but what kind of dialogue are we creating? And what kind of world do we expect to come from that?

Most Americans aren't nearly as polarized as the media suggest. Most of us aren't at some mushy middle point either. Talk—really sit down and talk—with your neighbors, colleagues, friends, and here is what you'll find:

There is a hunger in this country for a new kind of politics.

There is a hunger for a politics that can take us beyond the usual venomous blame games in Washington, D.C.

There is a hunger for a politics that appreciates the genuine and often very reasonable concerns of the left and right, and builds on them toward something new.

There is a hunger for a politics that's idealistic but without illusions, a politics that dares to suggest real solutions to our biggest problems but doesn't lose touch with the often harsh facts on the ground.

There is a hunger for a politics that expresses us as we really are—practical *and* visionary, mature *and* imaginative, sensible *and* creative, all at once.

Our politics today doesn't express either our practical, grounded side or our visionary, creative side.

It is all about the short term, not the long term. It is all about blaming others for our problems, not about turning our problems into opportunities by addressing them in the forthright, imaginative ways you know we can.

The recent Democratic presidential debates don't augur well for a different kind of politics, or a positive future. If the candidates agree about anything, it's that our problems all stem from—the Republicans! And, of course, the Republicans take the opposite view.

Even the usual opponents of politics as usual seem more interested in bashing cartoon enemies than crafting a better future. Michael Moore's current left-wing bestseller, *Dude, Where's My Country?*, is devoted to blaming a diabolical economic elite for nearly everything wrong with this country and the world. It preaches a sort of proletarian, or hippie, McCarthyism: if you wear wing-tip shoes, you're suspect.

Meanwhile, Laura Ingraham's current right-wing bestseller, *Shut Up and Sing*, blames an arrogant cultural elite for everything that's gone wrong. Her book includes uncomplimentary color pictures of the evil ones—people like Ramsey Clark and Madonna—so when you lose interest in the staccato prose you can stare at the photos and work up some hate.

What is a good person to do? Ignore the noise.

In real life, you don't have to be a hard-left militant or hard-right militant to change the world. There's a third alternative now to politics as usual—radical middle politics.

In this book I'll tell you about that emerging new politics and sensibility. And I'll show you that, if you share this perspective, you are not alone.

Again and again in these pages, you'll discover that many Americans want us to move away from the politics of us-against-them, and toward a politics that combines the best of the left and the right, and goes beyond them.

More than two centuries ago, Benjamin Franklin wanted us to invent a uniquely American politics that served ordinary people by creatively borrowing from all points of view. It's not too late for us to listen to him.

Many nonpartisan or post-partisan Americans are asking basic questions, now, that can move us toward a new and more relevant politics. Here are four I've put front and center in this book:

- How can we give ourselves more choices in life?
- How can we give everyone a fair start in life?
- How can we maximize our potential as human beings?
- How can we be of use to the developing world?

At the radical middle, we're not only asking these questions. We're proposing concrete answers—practical solutions to the most pressing issues of our time.

For example, with just a little bit of cleverness and imagination, and a willingness to borrow, humbly, from neoliberals, neopopulists, neoconservatives, and transformationalists alike, we can make ourselves energy independent within ten years.

We can create a universal health care system that's preventive, and affordable, and not government-run.

We can provide affirmative action for all economically disadvantaged Americans.

We can create corporations we'd actually enjoy working for.

We can make globalization work for everyone.

We can keep terrorists away from our shores—and at the same time come to passionate grip with the causes of terrorism.

I've woven these ideas and more into this book. But I also tell you how millions of us have begun actually working for the mature, creative, 21st-century America these ideas foreshadow.

For example: we're figuring out how to bring our radical middle values into our workplaces. We're getting involved in neighborhood groups that emphasize collaborative problem solving. We're pushing professional associations and national citizen groups to the radical middle.

Some national groups are there already. Take Environmental Defense. It is one of our most principled environmental advocacy groups and employs more scientists than any other. At the same time, it's one of the few environmental groups that's willing to work proudly and openly with major corporations like McDonald's and FedEx, as well as with governments and community groups. As a result, it's come under heavy fire from the political left. Also as a result, it's often able to forge "radical middle" solutions that work for everyone.

Or take Ashoka. Like many nonprofits, it sends money to developing countries. But it sends money not to poor people, or governments, or other nonprofits, but to "social entrepreneurs"—teachers and doctors and activists and other individuals who've come up with innovative ideas for how to serve their societies. And it doesn't just send money. It gives its recruits great training and consulting, and puts them in touch with each other, and keeps up with them for years. Is Ashoka a charity or a unique sort of business venture? The best answer is both. It is a radical middle development model.

In this book, I steer you to over 50 such groups. And I won't consider this book a success unless you're tempted to join one.

You'll soon see that this book is a bit more personal than most political books. Radical middle politics comes from the heart as well as the head, and I saw no reason to disguise that.

You'll find fewer references to sources here than you'll find in most political books, but don't let that fool you. This book draws on over a thousand published sources. To keep it uncluttered and short, I've avoided footnotes, but you can Google up most of my sources based on information in the text. And my most important sources and the most pertinent groups are always listed (annotated, even) in the "Resources" section at the end of each chapter.

I hope you'll take advantage of these lists to learn more. This book is about where we're going (knock on wood), not the same old same old. It is meant to be a beginning, not an end.

Washington, D.C.
January 5, 2004

PART ONE
THE EMERGING
NEW POLITICS

1

A CREATIVE
AND PRACTICAL POLITICS

S LOWLY AT FIRST, and now in growing numbers, from kitchen tables to nonprofit organizations to corporate boards, Americans are turning away from the politics of bickering and division and working out a new politics—a politics of creative problem solving.

It would have us take the best from the political left and right, and come up with something new that serves us all.

It would have us come up with solutions to public issues that are thoughtful enough, clever enough, and inclusive enough, to bring people and factions together.

It doesn't have an official name yet. So I hope you'll bear with me and allow me to christen it "radical middle" politics.

You can describe it as a political point of view and a growing political movement, but it's not necessarily so elaborate. It's an attitude, an impulse, a mood. You'll know it when you see it.

If you see pundits shouting half-truths at each other on cable TV—or demonstrators with simplistic slogans on their picket signs ("Bush the Baby Killer's Helper!", "Stop the Racist War!")—or politicians spending years in cushy office without ever finding the courage to propose real, long-term, sustainable solutions to our most pressing problems—then you know you're very far from the radical middle.

But when someone on your school board suggests that schools need better teachers and that that means giving school principals the right to hire and fire teachers and set their pay—then the radical middle is in plain view. You've got someone coming up with a bold and constructive goal (better teachers), and a practical means for carrying it out (empowering individual schools).

When a community activist addresses a problem in your community—and instead of scapegoating government or business, proposes a solution to the problem that involves working with city hall or the business community—then you're seeing radical middle politics first hand. Because the radical middle is not about bashing government or business. It is about learning to listen to everyone, learning to work with everyone, and learning to build on everyone's best insights.

When a politician proposes an approach to universal health care that would cover everyone—every single American—and would take full advantage of preventive and alternative medicine, but would build on privately run insurance plans, then you're seeing radical middle politics. Here again, you've got a bold, radical goal (universal health care), but you're getting there without setting up a bureaucratic National Health Service. And you're saving money by creatively building on many people's interest in preventive and alternative health care measures.

When at your workplace you're invited to help create and discuss a series of future scenarios for your company and later invited to help implement the most promising one or ones—then you're seeing radical middle politics. The radical middle is not just government programs. It's corporations, labor unions, and many other institutions adapting to the fact that many Americans are becoming increasingly capable and knowledgeable (and bored to tears at jobs that don't require initiative or allow for participation).

When a politician gives a damn about people in developing countries—and not only gives a damn, but proposes real help that won't bust the bank, such as providing small loans to farmers or opening U.S. markets to fledgling manufacturers—then you're seeing radical middle politics. Because it's a politics for caring people.

When your kid comes home carrying a huge new textbook about global history, a book that helps him or her see the U.S. as neither a Racist Imperialist Demon nor God's Gift to Mankind, but in glorious cultural, economic, environmental, and political context—then you're seeing radical middle politics. Because it's a politics for people with the imagination and the humility to see themselves as part of a much larger whole.

And if your best friend comes to you saying she'd like to run for office on a platform consisting of creative policy prescriptions that are nevertheless very grounded and responsible (and affordable), and wondering whether you might be interested in helping run her campaign—then you're not only seeing radical middle politics. You are being invited to help create it.

For it is by no means a "done deal." It is a politics in process.

Liberalism and conservatism, Marxism and anarchism, are all European political philosophies. Radical middle politics—with its combination of quintessentially American creativity and quintessentially American pragmatism—may turn out to be our first home-grown political philosophy.

To succeed, though, it needs your efforts. And the efforts of all caring Americans.

IDEALISM WITHOUT ILLUSIONS

Politics is stuck in America today. We need to break through the stale debates and self-serving non-solutions that are coming from both political parties, and we need to do it without ending up at the "mushy middle," where there's no direction or principle.

That's where the radical middle comes in.

The radical middle is an attempt to break out of that stuckness in a fresh and principled way. It consists of everyone who's bold and yet savvy enough to want idealism *without* illusions—a fresh and hopeful vision that doesn't fall into the trap, as many leftists do, of looking back to chestnuts from the counter-culture of the Sixties and Seventies, such as socialist economics or neo-anarchist democracy or a wildly optimistic view of human nature.

The radical middle looks to the present and future. It says we live in a new era dominated by high technology and "knowledge work" and disappearing borders, and we need a politics that's appropriate for our new time. A politics that's "radical" in the sense that it addresses fundamental public policy issues in ways that are honest and imaginative and creative—but "middle" in the sense that it doesn't aspire to overthrow corporate capitalism or representative democracy. It is committed to finding practical, humane, and thoroughgoing answers to the very real problems of American institutions and corporate capitalism.

Call it the experienced person's alternative to politics-as-usual and bitter street protest.

Its advocates tend to be subtle and imaginative, rational and creative, sensible and forward-looking, pragmatic and visionary. "Balance" is not a wimp-word to those at the radical middle; on the contrary, it can be high praise.

Some political movements barely twiddle the dials of the status quo. Others confuse idealism and hope with trying to breathe new life into the crude anti-Establishment verities of the Sixties. The radical middle is different still. It traffics in thoughtful idealism and informed hope—idealism without illusions.

FOUR KEY VALUES

The radical middle movement is phenomenally diverse. But when you look at what everyone who might be called radical middle is saying and doing, you'll discover we share four goals. I like to call them our Four Key Values:

1. maximize choices for every American (and for the U.S. as a whole) as much as possible;
2. guarantee a fair start in life to every American;
3. maximize every American's human potential as much as possible;
4. be of genuine help to everyone in the developing world.

Put these values together and you can see how the radical middle draws holistically on our entire political tradition. Each value is a sort of updated version of an aspect of our 18th-century political heritage—liberty, equality, happiness, and fraternity, respectively. You could say that each value pays homage to (even as it radically updates) a different industrial-era perspective—conservative, liberal, humanistic, and evangelical, respectively. Don't tell the ACLU, but you can even see aspects of the Christian faith (or virtually any world faith) in them—I would say peace, grace, joy, and love, respectively.

The Four Key Values are not just provocative abstractions. You can use them to identify what more and more of us are beginning to want, and why:

Maximize choices.

In the postindustrial era, we've become better educated, more expressive, more self-reliant, and more individualistic. That's a fancy way of saying we've learned more than our Greatest-Generation parents, we feel freer to say (and hold out for) what we want, we're less haplessly dependent on our jobs and our spouses, and we spend more time consciously shaping and re-shaping our personal identities. As a result, we want public policies that can provide us with many choices in life, rather than one-size-fits-all government programs.

Take health care. Many of us are beginning to envision a universal health care system that would allow us to choose among a kaleidoscope of preventive and alternative health care options.

Or take law reform. Those of us at the radical middle would see to it that many affordable choices were offered to folks in trouble— from innovative kinds of mediation, to dramatically expanded small claims courts, to hands-on "problem-solving courts."

Besides expanding people's choices, we'd have the government itself expand its policy choices. Take energy. Instead of continuing to be dangerously dependent on Middle Eastern oil, or making a heroic stab in the dark at the most promising unproven energy alternative c. 2004, we'd have the government provide a substantial amount of support to each of seven very different energy paths on a continuing basis—conservation, renewables, "clean" fossil fuels, hydrogen, nuclear, biobased fuels, and lifestyle change. We'd bring each to the fore whenever each is ready to meet our energy needs cheaply and safely.

Give everyone a fair start.

For Democrats and Republicans, this is a largely rhetorical commitment. For radical middle thinkers, it's an absolutely essential commitment. Almost a choiceless one. No caring person wants to feel they've gotten as far as they have because others were held back.

What can be done? Plenty, once you see things with the imaginative but practical eye of the radical middle thinker-activist. From preschool through high school, we can pay maximum attention to providing kids with the Number One Thing they need in order to learn—competent and inspired and empowered teachers.

To give every economically deprived American a fair start, we can provide two things, and the sooner the better. First, a decent-paying job for every able-bodied person willing to work. (Government wouldn't necessarily have to provide the jobs—subsidies to private firms might suffice.) That means every kid would grow up in a home with at least one responsible, working parent in the economic mainstream. Second, we'd have government contribute to "individual development accounts" for every poor child. These could lead to one-time disbursements of $20,000 or more once the child reaches 18.

In higher education, we'd replace race-based affirmative action with affirmative action for the truly disadvantaged of every color and ethnicity. Why should the sons and daughters of elite lawyers (who happen to be black or Hispanic) be given a leg up over the sons and daughters of Teamsters or single moms (who happen to be white or Asian)? Our value commitment is to fairness for individuals, and we reject the far left's apparent desire to see America officially turned into a balkanized battleground of competing racial groups.

Maximize human potential.
Pundits who enjoy seeing themselves as tough-minded like to sneer at the concept of "human potential." It is said to be murky, squishy, even New Age. In fact, as developed by master American psychologists like Erik H. Erikson and Howard Gardner, it may be the most vital concept to enter the political arena in our lifetimes. It proclaims that politics (or any human endeavor) is about more than the giving or getting of things. It is also about helping the human spirit flourish, or not flourish. It is about creating conditions for individual human beings to be constantly learning and growing.

Everyone I know at the radical middle is sensitive to this task and eager to take it on. For example, we'd help corporations become better places to work—and better corporate citizens—by changing their cultures in a humane direction. We'd do this directly, by bringing in experienced but visionary consultants. We'd also do it indirectly, by pushing for visionary laws and regulations.

We speak in a cautiously optimistic voice on biotechnology, as distinct from the fearful voice of the antiglobalists, in part because of the potential biotech holds for creating healthier crops and humans—a potential that's barely been tapped.

Many of us would go so far as to reinstate the draft and make it universal, with military, homeland security, and community service options. We value absolute freedom—but not absolutely. We also value the positive psychological and spiritual effects that a year or two of national service might have on young Americans.

Help the developing world.
The fourth value that defines those of us at the radical middle is that we're totally committed to helping other peoples around the world survive—and flourish. That doesn't mean we feel a need to send them billions of dollars of aid out of some vague sense of guilt. It does mean we want to do whatever we can to be of use to them.

One way we can help is by supporting what I call free trade with a conscience—that is, free trade that could benefit working people in developing nations. A North American or European market can often make a world of difference to farmers and small producers in Africa, Latin America, or Asia.

Another way we can help is by supporting intervention, including armed intervention, to prevent humanitarian catastrophes abroad. Despite the quasi-pacifist outlook of the traditional peace movement, many of us see the push for humanitarian armed intervention as the real peace movement of our time; over six million innocent people have died in civil (mostly genocidal) wars since the early 1990s.

As for terrorism, most of us support a two-track approach that typically runs afoul of left and right—one track seriously vigilant against the harm terrorists might do, the other track tough on the socioeconomic roots of terrorism, so tough that it envisions a Marshall Plan for developing countries combining emergency aid, special attention to education, and special attention to building up local and world-class enterprises.

So, there you have it: a quick overview of the Four Key Values of the radical middle. In Parts Two to Five below, I'll tell you more—much more—about the policies that could make those values real in this country today. And in Part Six I'll outline a political strategy that's consistent with them (and that's already being carried out in bits and pieces by radical middle activists)—a strategy that calls on us to work within the system rather than stand on the sidelines and feel simon-pure. But before we get into that, I want to spend the next two chapters telling you where all these radical middle ideas are coming from.

By and large, they're not coming from political intellectuals in universities. Nor are they coming from members of Congress. Nor are they coming from pale, sullen denizens of cafes in Paris and Berlin. Overwhelmingly, they're coming from busy, creative, and caring Americans like you and me.

RESOURCES

Texts

For other big-picture introductions to radical middle politics, see Ted Halstead and Michael Lind, *The Radical Center: The Future of American Politics* (2001), focusing on domestic issues; Matthew Miller, *The Two Percent Solution: Fixing America's Problems in Ways Liberals and Conservatives Can Love* (2003), also focusing on domestic issues; and Walter Truett Anderson, *All Connected Now: Life in the First Global Civilization* (2001), focusing on global issues.

For a British social-democratic version of radical middle, see Anthony Giddens, *The Third Way and Its Critics* (2000). For a radical middle communitarianism, see Amitai Etzioni, *Next: The Road to the Good Society* (2001). For an attempt by prominent left- and right-of-center policy analysts to make radical middle ideas palatable to elite policymakers, see Isabel Sawhill et al., *Updating America's Social Contract* (2000). For an African-American thinker with an arguably radical middle perspective, see John McWhorter, *Losing the Race* (2000), and his recent political essays, accessible online. For an arguably radical middle conservatism, see the Manhattan Institute's *City Journal*, accessible online.

The article that put the term "radical middle" on the American cultural map was Joe Klein's cover story "Stalking the Radical Middle," *Newsweek* (25 September 1995).

2

THE CARING PERSON

I WAS SITTING ON A SUBWAY TRAIN the other day in my hometown of Washington, D.C., paying rapt attention—as I often do—to the sights and sounds around me. In front of me, a man in his 50s was reading psychologist Robert Karen's wonderful book *The Forgiving Self: The Road from Resentment to Connection*. Just behind me, two people were talking about the interesting work they were doing at the Agency for International Development. A young woman sat down next to me, opened her tattered carrying bag—and whipped out a copy of the Kaplan study guide to the Law School Admission Test (LSAT). I told her I'd taken the LSAT, and we got to talking about the kinds of things she hoped to do in law. None of them had much to do with making a lot of money.

Sometimes I can't help thinking that the radical middle perspective is not only on the verge of becoming an explicit and enticing new political point of view in this country. Sometimes I think that most of us already share it—in bits and pieces of course, and not usually consciously.

And I have good company in this. Some of our best pollsters would agree with me. So would some of our best social scientists. They're beginning to describe an increasingly visible American whom I've christened the "caring person." Of course, there have always been caring people in this country, and many hold traditional political views. But the emergence of the caring person as a model of a new political way of being in the world is the most exciting and hopeful development of my lifetime—not least of all because the caring person effortlessly embodies the Four Key Values of the radical middle.

A RADICAL MIDDLE MAJORITY?

The radical middle perspective isn't a creation of scholars or activists or well-funded think tanks. Credible pollsters have found it's an emerging perspective of the American people—in some ways already a majority perspective.

Increasingly, we appear to be—on many issues—quintessentially radical middle: subtle *and* imaginative, rational *and* creative, sensible *and* forward-looking. In addition, we appear to be willing (even eager) to borrow or combine good ideas from all parts of the political spectrum. By contrast, most of our politicians—and, sadly, many of our activists—appear to be simplistic, unimaginative, and woodenly partisan. Just think of Al Gore and George W. Bush during the 2000 Presidential campaign; or any recent statement from Accuracy in Media or the National Organization for Women.

The Founding Fathers worried mightily about how to keep "the people's" unsophisticated political passions in check. But, increasingly, it's "the people" who seem savvy and visionary. And it's our elected (or self-chosen) representatives who seem drawn to wildly partisan half-truths.

Nonpartisan polls bear out the public's pragmatic and imaginative bent—particularly sophisticated, in-depth surveys from Andrew Kohut's Pew Research Center, Steven Kull's Center on Policy Attitudes, Alan Wolfe and Maria Poarch's Middle Class Morality Project, and Daniel Yankelovich's Public Agenda Online.

What all those pollsters are finding is a public that's much more thoughtful, much more creative—and much more caring—than jaded pundits care to admit. It is not the public of the antiglobalists' fantasies; for example, most of us (correctly, I think) support free trade and biotechnology, which the antiglobalists ardently oppose. But neither is it the public of the mind-numbing rhetoric of the Democratic and Republican parties.

What I am calling the creative public, Kohut calls the "complex" public. "Simply put," he says, "the public's view can't be put simply."

Kull calls us the "rational" public. Yankelovich celebrates our eager-
ness to blend facts, feelings, and values. Wolfe claims we're
"nonideological" and "deeply pragmatic" but also surprisingly "cos-
mopolitan."

The reason these pollsters are impressed with the American public these days is no mystery. It has everything to do with how we've
performed in their polls. Repeatedly, we've come across more
thoughtfully than the pollsters expected. Repeatedly, we've defied
traditional partisan lines. In the process, we've often come across as
radical middle:

Maximize choices for everyone.
Two-thirds of us think health care is a right that should be guaranteed by the government (the traditional left-wing position). But most
of us do not want the government to be the only health care player;
57 percent of us oppose national health care in which the government is the only insurer (the traditional conservative position). What
the public appears to be saying is: give us universal health care, but
give us plenty of choices within any such plan.

Give everyone a fair start.
What the left wants in today's schools is smaller class sizes; what the
right wants is more testing. What the public wants is a third thing:
great teachers. A majority of us would raise teachers' pay, and an
overwhelming 89 percent of us would require all teachers to pass
competency exams—a requirement many teachers and their unions
oppose. Clearly the public is neither pro-teacher nor anti-union so
much as it is pro-pupil, as it should be.

Maximize human potential.
Over 90 percent of us support corporate reform, but our goal is to
make corporations better places to work and better members of society; it is not to cut corporations down to size or make them creatures
of the state. Wolfe says we believe in a "balanced," "moral" capitalism. Similarly, most of us support a ban on human cloning, but our
motives aren't punitive toward biotech. Nearly 60 percent of us favor
the cloning of human organs or body parts that can then be used in

medical transplants. Our motive in both corporate reform and cloning appears to be humanistic—wanting to do what's best to enhance people's lives.

Help the developing world.
Despite many politicians' and activists' cries to "Buy American!" and despite a constant undertow of calls to cut back on America's role in the world, most of us now appear to want America to be a stand-up member of the global community. Over 60 percent of us are convinced free trade will benefit our children. A stunning 77 percent of us think there are times when other countries have the right to intervene to protect people from their own governments. Nearly 80 percent of us would address terrorism in part by helping poor countries develop their economies.

If all these positions—radical middle to their core—don't reflect the minds and hearts of a caring people, then I don't know which do.

COMING OF THE CREATIVE CLASS

Pollsters have established that radical middle views are emergent—even, in some cases, dominant. But where are those views coming from? Who holds them, and why?

By and large, they're not coming to us from far-sighted politicians or a suddenly visionary media. They're coming from a deeper source. Who we are as a people is changing—and that's inexorably changing what we want and what we value.

As the 20th century began, most Americans were farmers and industrial workers. For the last four decades, a plurality of us have been service workers. An economy primarily dependent on farmers, industrial workers, and service workers will favor such norms as conformity, predictability, loyalty, and fitting in, and it's not hard to see why. Those are the qualities you need in an industrial-era workforce.

It is not a matter of good people and bad people. Nor is it a matter of capitalists "oppressing" the rest of us. It is just that, if you want an industrial-era economy to work, then you need people to show up at work at a certain set time, perform repetitive tasks without too much acting out or daydreaming, and happily consume the standard-ized products the economy is great at churning out.

There are advantages to industrial-era rigidity. If you get good at it, you can help win two world wars and one cold war. Also, schooling can be mostly by rote, which makes it a lot easier to do. And families tend to stick together longer, since everybody's roles are more defined; which is another way of saying that everybody's choices are more limited.

As a young man, I spent some time in the industrial economy, so I don't romanticize it the way some academics and antiglobalists do. One of my jobs was working at an enormous cannery in Oregon as a member of the Teamsters Union. Dozens of cans a minute came rat-tling down long chutes, and I had to stand there and pick up four at a time, four at a time, four at a time, endlessly, and deftly place them in cardboard boxes which some other happy guy would lug out to the boxcars forever waiting in back. By the time mid-morning rolled around, tears would involuntarily be rolling down my cheeks. Tears of boredom. The pay was good though.

I had another industrial-era job handling legal documents at the land titles office in Toronto. That job was less stressful, to put it mildly. I'd fold the documents in the mornings, and spend the afternoons put-ting them in hundreds of wooden drawers and army-green filing cabi-nets. About 15 guys worked there doing similarly interesting things.

Although one of my industrial-era jobs was "blue collar" and the other "white collar," the dominant subjects of conversation were exactly the same at both: sports and sex. In that order. Our limited per-sonal repertoires perfectly mirrored the narrow, suffocating nature of our supposed life's work, which most of us never thought of leaving or even humanizing except in our wildest dreams. By the age of 30, most of us felt with a terrible certainty that our best days were behind us.

The industrial era is on its way out now, mercifully, I'd say, and in its place is what social scientists are calling the knowledge era. It still includes farms, factories, and offices, of course. But most of the work done there is done far more creatively and systemically—in part by making maximum use of high technology, and in part by making maximum use of employees' own unique experiences and knowledge. To further enhance creativity, an ever-increasing amount of work is being handled by independent individuals and hyper-specialized small organizations.

So instead of hand-loading cans off assembly lines now, we do it with the help of extraordinary machines. Instead of shuffling around millions of documents, we get good at computers. Instead of impersonally processing medical patients, we train doctors and nurses to listen to their patients, and pick their remedies with exquisite sensitivity to each patient's wants and needs.

The knowledge era is, in sum, so different from the industrial era that it requires an entirely different sort of person to carry out its tasks.

If the industrial era favored norms like conformity and loyalty—norms that helped industrial-era institutions function well—then the knowledge era favors norms that help knowledge-oriented institutions function well. Our most essential knowledge-era norms include creativity, individuality, self-expression, curiosity about self and others and world, self-reliance, social service, and enjoyment of—not just toleration of—differences.

Put those norms together and you get the kind of person who might feel comfortable with the Four Key Values of the radical middle. In fact, you get the kind of person who might fight for them—just as working people once fought for socialism or the welfare state.

Most of us aren't there yet. According to urban economist Richard Florida, 43 percent of the workforce consists of the service class, and 27 percent consists of the industrial working class. Only 30 percent consists of what many call "knowledge workers" and Florida prefers to call the "creative class." These include people in science, engineering, architecture, education, the arts, and entertainment, as well as professionals in such fields as business, finance, marketing, law, journalism, and health care.

But that figure is up tenfold from what it was 100 years ago, and it's continuing to climb. And it would be the height of arrogance to assume that, just because people are in the service or industrial sectors, they haven't adopted many of the norms that have fueled the creative class and the value commitments of the radical middle. You can even argue—as does futurist labor scholar Arthur Shostak—that creativity and self-expression are just as necessary in the service and industrial sectors now as they are in the knowledge sector.

Still, it's probably fair to say that knowledge workers, aka the creative class, constitute our most important class now—since our economy runs on knowledge now and depends for its lifeblood on creativity and innovation. As a result, the norms of the creative class—which many in the industrial era looked down upon as bohemian or worse—are becoming the accepted norms for society as a whole.

THE CARING PERSON

The rise of knowledge workers and the creative class represents more than a change in lifestyle. It represents a change in what significant numbers of Americans want for themselves, their country, and the world.

Put the new norms of the creative class together and you get a new model or archetype of the Good American, whom I like to call the "caring person."

The caring person is the carrier of radical middle politics, just as the bourgeoisie was the carrier of classical liberalism and the working class was the carrier of socialism (in Europe) and the welfare state (in the U.S.).

To see this clearly, it's helpful to look at three competing archetypes of the Good American—not just the caring person, but two archetypes from the industrial era that are still very much with us, the "self-aggrandizing individual" and the "self-sacrificing individual."

We've all met versions of the self-aggrandizing individual. Self-aggrandizers are ambitious strivers. They get their primary identity from their occupation and the social status associated with that. They believe passionately in the concept of freedom, especially the freedom to accumulate material possessions. When Democrats try to picture Republicans, they often think in terms of the self-aggrandizing individual.

We've all met versions of the self-sacrificing individual, too. Self-sacrificing individuals are not personally ambitious—and when they are, they try to hide it. They get their primary identity from their ethnic, racial, or religious affiliation or sexual orientation. They believe passionately in social justice and occasionally even fight for it. When Republicans try to picture Democrats, they often think in terms of the self-sacrificing individual.

The caring person is an archetype that embodies the norms of knowledge workers and the creative class. Caring persons may or may not be personally ambitious, but they want their jobs to provide them with opportunities for personal growth *and* social relevance. They get their primary identity from the lifestyle choices they make and the values they consciously choose. They are equally committed to personal freedom *and* social justice, self-development *and* social change. When caring persons try to picture Republicans and Democrats, they often think in terms of the self-aggrandizing individual and the self-sacrificing individual. But then they mentally kick themselves—because they know they can't get anywhere if they caricature their political opponents.

Caring persons are far more common than you might think. The wonderful writers, scholars, and activists I draw on in this book are all, by and large, caring persons. The administrators turning our professional schools into social change incubators are caring persons. The consultants helping transnational corporations become more sensitive to the needs of consumers and poor people in developing nations are caring persons.

If your child's elementary school teacher volunteers to stay late to provide special tutoring, then that teacher is a caring person— whatever the local teachers' union may think. If your son or daughter joins the military because he or she wants to help America defend itself and develop the capacity to stop genocidal wars in developing nations, then he or she is without a doubt a caring person.

Who says we have no heroes today? Many caring persons are just that, though they're not often in the camera's eye.

The creative class and those who share its norms is expanding. Which is why the caring person is emerging. Which is why the radical middle is on the march.

RESOURCES

Texts

For intimations of a radical middle majority, see Alan Wolfe, *One Nation, After All* (1998); Andrew Kohut, "Simply Put, The Public's View Can't Be Put Simply," *Washington Post* (29 September 2002); and I. M. Destler, "The Reasonable Public and the Polarized Policy Process," in Anthony Lake, ed., *The Real and the Ideal* (2001) or available online.

For the rise of knowledge workers and the social and political implications of that, see Richard Florida, *The Rise of the Creative Class* (2000), a general overview; David Brooks, *Bobos in Paradise* (2000), a wonderfully written conservative take on the phenomenon, and broadly sympathetic; and John Judis and Ruy Teixeira, "Majority Rules," *The New Republic* (5 August 2002), a liberal take.

There are many handbooks for caring persons. Among my favorites: Esther Dyson, *Release 2.1: A Design for Living in the Digital Age* (1998); Warren Farrell, *Father and Child Reunion* (2001); Robert Fuller, *Somebodies and Nobodies: Overcoming the Abuse of Rank* (2003); Robert Karen, *The Forgiving Self: The Road from Resentment to Connection* (2001), which makes a cameo appearance in this chapter; James Levine, *Working Fathers: New Strategies for Balancing Work and Family* (1997); Michael Segell, *Standup Guy: Manhood After Feminism* (1999); Pat Summitt with Sally Jenkins, *Reach for the Summit* (1998); and William Ury, *Getting to Peace: Transforming Conflict at Home, at Work, and in the World* (1999).

3

JOURNEY TO THE
RADICAL MIDDLE

AT THE AGE OF 19 I led a coup against the tiresome old so-cialist-intellectual leadership of my college chapter of Stu-dents for a Democratic Society (SDS), at Harpur College in upstate New York. I wish I could report my success was due to my finely developed political program. Alas, it was my propensity for reckless action that turned folks on. Suddenly, instead of sitting around talking about What Would Marx or Lenin Do?, we were one blue streak of incendiary speeches, anti-draft actions, antiwar rallies, over-the-top manifestos, and threatened curfew strikes.

My "action faction" wasn't just rebelling against the establish-ment. Although we considered ourselves revolutionaries (who didn't, in 1966?), we were also rebelling against the left and its dreary vision of noble workers and enforced equality. We sensed that a new gener-ation of college-educated professionals, managers, and white-collar workers would soon be in position to build a phenomenally diverse and exciting new world consisting of many more choices for individ-uals and nations.

Our vision was proto–radical middle. But we hadn't a clue how to articulate it. In the wee hours we'd go off searching for writers who were speaking to us, but we'd always come up empty.

There were a few far-seeing commentators, most notably busi-ness consultant Peter Drucker. As far back as the Fifties he was writing about the rise of knowledge workers and the society-altering potential of their norms and values—creativity, self-reliance, self-

expression, and all the rest of it. A couple of us paged through
Drucker, but in our 19-year-old, revolution-addled wisdom we were
not impressed. He was just a business guy, probably wore wing-tip
shoes. You couldn't tell from his writing if he was liberal or conservative. And he wanted to reinvent capitalism, for crying out loud. All
the really cool folks we knew wanted to destroy capitalism, not per-
petuate it.

FRANKLIN TO PETERS TO YOU

My burning desire to destroy capitalism (and The System for which it
stands) led me down many blind alleys. And by the way, if you came of
age in the Sixties, were you immune? Over the last 40 years, U.S. political activists have spent billions of person-hours trying to tease relevant insights out of communists, anarchists, and anyone
deconstructionist and vaguely paranoid. Meanwhile, radical middle
politics lay there for the taking, thanks to the spadework of Drucker
and some others.

In a sense, it's always been here. If Thomas Jefferson is the liberals' (and libertarians') Founding Father, and George Washington is
the conservatives', and Tom Paine is the radicals', then Benjamin
Franklin is the radical middle's.

He was extraordinarily practical—ran a fabulously successful
printing business for 20 years, started innumerable community im-
provement associations. At the same time, he was extraordinarily
creative—invented bifocals, the lightning rod, and the Franklin
stove. He was a man of principle—opposed colonial tax policies that
would have benefited him personally, became a leader in the fight
against slavery. Yet synthesis and healing were an art with him. He
became our most ardent champion of religious tolerance. And better
than anyone else at the Constitutional Convention, he was able to
get the warring factions and wounded egos to transcend their differences and come up with a Constitution for the ages.

Franklin was hardly alone in the tenor of his views. You could even
say that the years from 1770 to 1790 were the years of our first great
radical middle political movement. Surely the single most important
and glorious radical middle document is the *Federalist Papers*
(1787–89)—James Madison, Alexander Hamilton, and John Jay's

collected newspaper columns arguing that the freshly drafted Constitution should be ratified by the 13 states. In their eyes, the Constitution was both extraordinarily practical and admirably visionary, and their defense of it often relied on a characteristically radical middle blend of realism and vision.

Almost two centuries later, in the mid-1970s, forces began gathering for a second great radical middle political movement, the one we can see now on the horizon.

I was disillusioned; we all were. Martin Luther King, Jr.'s and Robert F. Kennedy's assassinations were still reverberating in our souls; the New Left political movement had collapsed; even traditional liberalism had been discredited (because many social problems turned out to be impervious to the traditional liberal solution of "Just spend more money"). There was a hunger for new political forces that could challenge the far right and the big government left. Four forces appeared that are still with us, and each has something vital to contribute to the emerging radical middle movement:

- **Neoliberals** proved you could be liberal on social and economic issues while at the same time lambasting outdated big-government policies and inefficient government bureaucracies, getting tough on crime, and going to bat for entrepreneurs.

  Although there were some neoliberals in Congress (including Tim Wirth, Paul Tsongas, and Gary Hart), the most influential neoliberal was Charlie Peters, recently retired editor of the *Washington Monthly*. Peters had been an evaluator of Peace Corps programs, and he thought, Why not start a magazine, written by talented young journalists (on tiny Peace-Corps-style stipends), that would evaluate all government programs and doings with the same fine-tooth comb? Out of years of that kind of painstaking, unpretentious, real-world-only journalism came the neoliberal philosophy (Peters coined the term himself, in 1979). The Democratic Leadership Council, an influential group of Democratic Party officeholders and operatives that for years has been trying to get the party to act more "centrist," is often seen as neoliberal. But the poll-driven centrism of the DLC has little in common with the principled,

liberalism-plus-common-sense perspective that Peters and his
young journalists wrought.
- **Neopopulists** proved that issues of social and economic class
  were still very much with us.

  Some neopopulists came across like capitalist-bashers from
  the 1930s. But others proposed innovative, forward-looking, and
  admirably concrete remedies with a minimum of rhetoric. For
  example, attorney Richard Kahlenberg proposed making every
  public school racially and economically diverse. Social scientists
  like Richard Freeman, Roberto Unger, and Cornel West proposed giving young people large one-time financial grants when
  they turned 18. And the Jobs for All Coalition proposed a variety
  of ways to ensure that every able-bodied person could find a
  well-paying job.
- **Neoconservatives** proved that you didn't have to abandon your
  commitment to opportunity for all just because you finally understood that capitalism is more economically efficient than socialism, and personal responsibility a more efficacious outlook than a
  bottomless sense of entitlement and rage. They also proved, for
  better and worse, that national security requires a strong and sup-
  ple military.

  Although extreme neocons like Charles Murray and Richard
  Perle garnered most of the headlines, a more interesting set of
  neocons lurked beneath the radar screen. Political scientist
  Lawrence Mead hammered out an approach to public assistance
  that would have guaranteed generous payments to needy Americans so long as they met certain behavioral requirements, such as
  working or staying in school or attending job-training classes. International development expert Lawrence Harrison argued that if
  nations want to prosper, they have no choice but to adopt Ben
  Franklinesque cultural values like frugality, investment, future-
  focus, work as central to the good life (not a burden), education
  as the key to progress, and merit as central to advancement. The
  National Endowment for Democracy, brainchild of neocon labor
  leaders, made and continues to make hundreds of grants each
  year to pro-democracy groups in developing countries.

• **Transformationalists** proved that many of the passions of the counter-culture were essential to a brighter future—among them, women's rights, racial healing, gay rights, the environment, holistic health, nutrition, animal rights, the fate of other cultures and peoples, and (not least) the psychological and spiritual well-being of Americans.

Few national politicians express a purely transformational point of view today. Congressman and 2004 Presidential candidate Dennis Kucinich (D-Ohio) comes closest, except he's probably even more clearly in the neopopulist camp. But transformational ideas and writers continue to deeply influence Americans from every walk of life. Magazines ranging from Michael Lerner's proudly intellectual *Tikkun* (a Hebrew word meaning "to mend, repair, and transform the world") to the breathlessly with-it *Utne Reader* continue to propagate not just the ideas but the spirit of the old counter-culture. Self-help writers with a transformational edge, such Jack Canfield, Wayne Dyer, Annie Gottlieb, Jean Houston, Dean Ornish, Scott Peck, Terrence Real, Neale Donald Walsch, and Marianne Williamson, reach millions of readers. Market researcher Paul Ray and psychologist Sherry Anderson make a credible case that 50 million "cultural creatives" are working their magic in the U.S. today—50 million people for whom the ideals of the old counter-culture burn brighter than ever.

The radical middle movement is a product of the lessons taught by all four strands above. True, some of those lessons are "radical," some "moderate," some "conservative"—but that is just my point. The radical middle is not another niche on the old left-right political spectrum. It is a genuinely new and remarkably broad-gauged political synthesis.

That synthesis is anything but abstract. In the next 12 chapters you'll see how radical middle thinking is leading to concrete and promising new approaches in areas ranging from economic policy to affirmative action to national defense. And that's nothing compared to what's on the horizon. The greatest radical middle thinkers will almost surely come from the back end of Generation X and the full run of Generation Y—basically, young people born from 1970 on. The radical middle is as natural to many of them as the air they breathe.

There's nothing defeatist or slacker-like about that group, but many of them appear to have had it up to here with the tired old self-definitions of 20th-century ideologues. Many of them appear to be as entrepreneurial as any libertarian might wish, as socially responsible as any progressive might wish, and as pragmatic as any moderate might wish—all at once.

They're optimists, they're team players, they accept properly constituted authority, they believe in science and technology and computers (and loathe Baby Boomers' supposed technophobia). At the same time, they value intelligence and creativity and independent thought. They are more radical middle than I can possibly hope to be.

A DIFFERENT ANIMAL

Although a radical middle movement is in the air, it should not be confused with the current antiglobalist movement. That is a different animal altogether.

The radical middle movement incorporates the best insights from the political left and right. The antiglobalist movement is far left and proud of it. The radical middle movement gives you idealism without illusions. The antiglobalist movement gives you idealism with illusions. Among them:

- the importance of being socialist (or anarchist);
- the idea that, in the long run, free trade is bad for us;
- the desirability of replacing representative democracy with direct democracy;
- the feeling that left-wing minority organizations or individuals shouldn't be criticized by white people;
- the desirability of a neo-pacifist foreign policy; and
- the notion of the perfectibility of human beings.

The radical middle movement would serve as America's moral voice. The antiglobalist movement is too alienated to serve as America's moral voice. Too often it sees white, mainstream America as something separate, no longer an "us" but a "them." Hard-left spokesman Michael Moore telegraphs this worldview when he writes, "You name the problem, the disease, the human suffering, or the abject misery visited upon millions, and I'll bet you ten bucks I can put a white face on it." A message T-shirt I've seen at antiglobalist rallies telegraphs this worldview even less subtly. It reads, "Normal People Scare Me."

My friend Mark Gerzon, facilitator of the first two "Bipartisan Congressional Retreats" (which drew nearly 200 members of Congress and their families to Hershey, Pa., in 1997 and 1999), says the hard left now essentially sees itself—and one can usefully view it—as a separate nation, which he calls "Disia." A nation of people constantly dissing others, and constantly on hair-trigger alert for instances of being dissed itself.

Millions of Americans want to make a difference in this world. Few of us want to waste our time engaging followers of Michael Moore over the moral significance of race; or followers of prominent antiglobalist David Korten over the question of whether capitalism is, as he's repeatedly claimed, a "cancer"; or followers of Naomi Klein, another antiglobalist hero, over whether "the system of centralized power itself" is the problem.

Most caring Americans are practical and creative, and want to implement practical and creative solutions to make our institutions better. They can find those solutions at the radical middle.

MY JOURNEY, AND YOURS

The written history of a political movement is usually very straightforward. Benjamin Franklin to Charlie Peters to you. In real life, though, everyone experiences that history much more chaotically. Your life may have recapitulated that history perfectly, yet you may have been only vaguely aware of the underlying trends pulling you in certain directions. You were probably much more aware—as I was—of very private enthusiasms and confusions, dreams and disillusionments, aspirations and regrets.

Certainly I had no idea, when I started out as an activist in the 1960s, that I had embarked on a long march to what I'm calling

the radical middle. All I knew was that my country had been brutal-
izing black people for hundreds of years, and had embarked on a
senseless and self-destructive war in Vietnam, and I'd never forgive
myself if I didn't do something. Anything.

So at age 18 I dropped out of school to go to Mississippi to work for
civil rights for the Student Nonviolent Coordinating Committee, out
of a tiny clapboard house in a little town called Holly Springs. Then,
without missing a beat, I was a VISTA volunteer—until they kicked
me out for refusing to sign a loyalty oath. Then I was kicked out of a
small Texas state university for the same reason. Then I was president
of my college SDS chapter, and 19 percent of the students eventually
joined, the highest percentage of student enrollment at any SDS chapter ever.

Life was proceeding faster than I could take it in. One day I gave
a speech proclaiming I would never, never, never kill people in Vietnam. Students wept. A couple of weeks later I rubbed my eyes and
found myself in Canada making good on my promise, and more. I
co-founded and ran the Toronto Anti-Draft Programme, the major
group helping young American draft resisters come to Canada—
meanwhile writing one of my generation's underground bestsellers,
the *Manual for Draft-Age Immigrants to Canada*.

It was all such a blur at the time. When the *Manual* was published I was all of 21. There were moments I didn't want to be anywhere but back in my hometowns (Moorhead, Minn. and Wichita
Falls, Tex.), enjoying an American boyhood free of rage over racism
and the war. Then again, there were moments I did more than I
should have to help people in and around the violent Weatherman
faction of SDS.

Eventually I got sick of the rhetoric that justified the violence,
and turned to "New Age" political pursuits. In a house trailer on an
island off the Vancouver coast, with the sea for my front yard and
Washington State's gorgeous Mount Baker shimmering in the dis-
tance and taunting me constantly (for I still couldn't return to the
U.S.), I wrote a book called *New Age Politics: Healing Self and Society* for a small Canadian publisher. After President Carter gave
amnesty in 1977 I took *New Age Politics* on the road, and the response at New Age gatherings, community events, fairs, bookstores,

living rooms, and college campuses kept me going for two whole years.

The book argued that a "third force" was possible in the United States though neither the highly confident mainstream nor the hunkered-down left cared to hear that message at the time.

Thanks to my long tour I was able to help organize a national "post-liberal, post-socialist" political organization called the New World Alliance (1979–1983, R.I.P.). I was one of its first staff members. Then I started and ran an idealistic national political newsletter called *New Options*. I didn't seek money from foundations—I really wanted the publication to be grassroots from the word go. So I started it with gifts and loans totaling $90,000 from hundreds of people I'd met on my travels. After ten years, *New Options* had become one of the largest independent political newsletters in the U.S.

I could have edited *New Options* forever. But, increasingly, I was becoming dissatisfied with my hyper-idealistic politics (and lifestyle). By day I'd preach decentralism, economic self-sufficiency, cooperative living, the death of hierarchy and the "great man." But when night fell I'd devour books on how to make free trade work for everyone, and prowl the West Wing of the National Gallery, full of world-class paintings by great men.

Finally I couldn't stand it anymore. I knew my views (and I personally) would benefit from engagement with the real world of commerce and professional ambition. The real world that was calling out to everyone so brassily in the early 1990s and that I'd avoided for so long. So I stopped *New Options* and enrolled at New York University School of Law, and enjoyed nearly every minute of it as only an experienced, mid-career student can. Later I worked on multi-million-dollar legal cases for an arbitrator-mediator and then a business litigator.

My lifestyle was suddenly, um, different: uniformed doormen at my Rockefeller Plaza office building were calling me "Mr. Satin" and wishing me good morning. And sometimes I was able to do good in the world. I remember one case where, after a few intense days of researching and writing, we were able to make one Fortune 500 company pay $6 million for what they'd done to the Hudson River. Most of the time I was sleepwalking, though. It wasn't the law's fault or even my employers' fault. I just needed to be doing something more like what I'd spent the first 25 years of my adult life doing.

On my long midnight walks from Rockefeller Center back to my fancy apartment, I decided I would not only return to political journalism and activism, I'd bring together the lessons I'd learned from the three very different parts of my life's journey.

From my New Left years I took a love of political struggle. From my New Age years I took a conviction that politics needs to be about more than endless struggle—that responsible human beings need to search for reconciliation and healing and mutually acceptable solutions. From my time in the legal profession I took an understanding (and it is no small understanding) that sincerity and passion are not enough—that to be truly effective in this world one needs to be credible and expert.

Putting all three lessons together brought me, inexorably, to the radical middle.

Now I make my living editing *Radical Middle*, a Washington, D.C.-based national political newsletter that keeps readers up on exciting new radical middle ideas and organizations.

Many Americans are living complicated lives now—few of us have moved through life in a straight line. I think many of us would benefit from trying to gather and synthesize the difficult political lessons we've learned over the course of our lives. When we do, I think many of us will realize we've ended up where I have—at the radical middle.

RESOURCES

Texts

For a recent summary of Peter Drucker's political views explicitly drawing on his ideas from the Sixties and Seventies, see Drucker, *Post-Capitalist Society* (1993). Other proto-radical middle thinkers from the pre-Reagan Era include Jane Jacobs (see especially *The Death and Life of Great American Cities*, 1961) and Heidi and Alvin Toffler (see especially *The Third Wave*, 1980).

For Benjamin Franklin as the radical middle Founding Father, treat yourself to Walter Isaacson's gorgeously written *Benjamin Franklin: An*

American Life (2003). Isaacson underlines Franklin's radical middle traits and sensibility.

Each of the four streams flowing into the radical middle is still going strong. For a fine recent neoliberal contribution, see James Fallows, *Breaking the News: How the Media Undermine American Democracy* (1996). For a neopopulist, see Nicholas Lemann, *The Big Test: The Secret History of the American Meritocracy* (1999). For a neoconservative, see Lawrence Harrison and Samuel Huntington, eds., *Culture Matters: How Values Shape Human Progress* (2000). For a transformational, see Paul Hawken et al., *Natural Capitalism: Creating the Next Industrial Revolution* (1999). For the radical middle potential of Gen-Y and the later Gen-Xers, see Neil Howe and William Strauss, *Millennials Rising: The Next Great Generation* (2000).

PART TWO

MAXIMIZE CHOICES
FOR EVERYONE

4

UNIVERSAL, PREVENTIVE HEALTH CARE: TOO SENSIBLE?

I F YOU EVER WORKED as a volunteer at a neighborhood health care clinic, as I did some years ago, you probably know all you really need to know about America's health care crisis.

Some of our clients were terrified—I mean, terrified—of the financial consequences of getting ill. I remember one client literally running out of our tiny, home-like office because the diagnosis he'd been given meant he'd likely have to spend most of his savings. Other clients wanted prescription drugs to cope with symptoms of their personal problems, ranging from poor diet and lack of exercise to loneliness, bottomless rage, and lack of self-esteem. Our beleaguered nurse-counselors did the best they could.

Today's health care crisis is so pressing that few politicians care to discuss it candidly. Do you know we now spend twice as much per capita on health care as the major European nations? We spend an astonishing 15 percent of our GNP on it—there's nothing miserly about our approach to health care. Yet health care premiums rose an additional 13.9 percent in 2003 (according to the Kaiser Family Foundation), over 40 million of us are uninsured, many of us are underinsured and going without care we need, and many of the rest of us are exasperated beyond measure by the poor quality of the attention and care we're getting from health care workers in organizational settings.

Congress's response has been unconscionable. For years its priority has been not to address these runaway problems, but to obsess about prescription drugs, which account for barely 10 percent of health care spending. And even in that area its plans are fiscally irresponsible and self-serving. Its bipartisan goal is to provide prescription drugs for senior citizens. Not financially strapped seniors, all seniors. Most seniors can afford their drugs, and a means test would strike anyone as fair; but an unusually high proportion of seniors vote.

And Congress isn't our only weakest link. For the last couple of years, left-leaning health care groups have been dragging a single-payer health care proposal around Capitol Hill like Linus dragging around his old blanket. Single-payer is where government finances all the medical costs of all the citizens of a nation (hence, government is the "single payer"). Canada has single-payer.

Most Americans don't support single-payer, though, and for good reason. The government would take over another 15 percent of the economy. Taxes would soar. People would no longer feel financial pressure to take personal responsibility for their own foolish health choices. The U.S. government's (or any big government's) efficiency is not something to write home about. Alternative care would become the equivalent of private or parochial school.

The time is right to devise a national health care plan drawing not on the tired nostrums of the left and right, but on the creative, pragmatic, and "both-and" spirit of the radical middle.

A radical middle health care plan would combine the traditional liberal policy goal of universal coverage for basic services with the efficiency of the private marketplace. In other words, it would make sure everyone had private insurance—not government insurance as per single-payer. And the plan would be expandable (for those who wanted to spend their own money on extra services), preventive, "integrative" (i.e., integrating conventional and alternative medicine), and public health oriented—partly to keep down costs. But partly to maximize choices for everyone, one of the key value commitments of the radical middle.

Americans are often closer to radical middle positions on issues than they are to traditional left- or right-wing positions, and that's certainly true here. Americans have expressed themselves loud and clear on the health care issue, and they appear to share the universal coverage / private insurance / preventive care / alternative care perspective of the radical middle:

- According to the nonpartisan Center on Policy Attitudes, most of us think health care is a right, like public education, that should be guaranteed by the government.
- At the same time, though, most of us are against significant tax increases toward that end. And most of us are against government health plans like single-payer.
- There's a "preventive care" explosion going on. With little prompting from Washington or Hollywood, we're exercising, running, flossing, using condoms, adopting vegetarian or semi-vegetarian diets, forswearing tobacco, etc., as never before.
- Increasingly, we're opting for "alternative" health care—chiropractic, herbal and Oriental medicine, homeopathy, etc. About 40 percent of us claim to have tried an alternative treatment, and at least two-thirds of us will be using one or more alternative treatments by 2010.

Putting these preferences together may seem daunting, but we're in luck. Hundreds of innovative health care scholars and practitioners—people the media rarely tell you about, like Clement Bezold, Rick Carlson, Leonard Duhl, James Gordon, David Kendall, and Grace-Marie Turner—are already on the case. Put their work together and you'll come up with an entire radical middle national health care system. . . .

MAKE IT UNIVERSAL—AND PRIVATE

If you want to drive a car, the government makes you buy private automobile insurance. You could be the safest driver in the world, but you'll still be required to have insurance—and for good reason. The taxpayers shouldn't have to cover you if you get into an accident and you're not insured.

A radical middle health care system would follow the automobile insurance model, while extending a helping hand to the poor. It would guarantee universal access to health care in three ways:

- by making every individual purchase private health insurance;
- by subsidizing those who can't afford insurance; and
- by crafting a "basic minimum package" of health benefits that every insurer would be required to offer at fixed cost.

The insurance.

A single-payer system would eliminate private insurance companies and make government responsible for financing basic medical coverage for the entire population. "Managed competition"—which is what Hillary Clinton called for in 1993—would make employers insure everyone, with small employers pooling together in incredibly complex arrangements (one reason her health care bill was over 1,300 pages long). The radical middle alternative is private, individual health care for all. Call it an "individual mandate," as distinct from Hillarycare's employer mandate.

Radical middle thinkers prefer an individual mandate because it fits our 21st-century lives and businesses better. "Median job tenure for all American workers 25 and older [is] down to five years," says Ted Halstead, thirtysomething founder of the New America Foundation, our first explicitly radical centrist think tank. "The model of lifetime employment with a single firm has given way to a model of serial employment with many firms. . . .

"Given these trends, maintaining our current employer-based health care [system is a bad proposition]. It leaves employees inherently insecure" because they're not only changing jobs but changing health care plans. And employers need to be freed from the "burden as serving as miniature welfare states, giving them the added flexibility they need in the new economy."

Better to make everyone buy private health insurance . . . just as everyone has to buy private insurance in order to drive.

Forcing people to buy insurance may appear to go against the radical middle value of maximizing choices. But going without health insurance imposes costs on others—and that diminishes *their* choices. Who do you think ultimately foots the bill when uninsured poor people (or uninsured thoughtless people) show up at hospital emergency rooms?

Of course, some people would refuse to sign up for health insurance—just as some people refuse to sign up for automobile insurance. But there are plenty of ways you could induce them to sign up. An annual tax penalty would probably be enough to bring your libertarian uncle on board. Or, more constructively, you could have the government enroll him "by default" into a private insurance plan—billing (or subsidizing) him according to his income as revealed on his tax return. It's not the worst thing in the world to force ornery old people and I-thought-it-could-never-happen-to-me young people to take responsibility for their health care coverage, especially since their refusal of responsibility makes everybody else pay more.

The subsidy.

Unfortunately, the government can't just wave a magic wand and mandate that everybody buy private health insurance. If we want truly universal coverage, then every single one of us has got to be able to afford it. A radical middle health care system would solve the affordability problem simply—with a government subsidy.

One of the first subsidy proposals—from Wharton School economists Patricia Danzon and Mark Pauly in the early 1990s—called for tax credits for health care expenditures by low-income people. If your health care expense exceeded your tax liability, you'd get the excess back from the IRS. Nice, nice. Radical middle thinkers at the New America Foundation have come up with an even more equitable subsidy proposal. They'd have us devote a certain percentage of our incomes to purchasing our own basic insurance plans, and have the government pick up the rest of the tab.

The basic benefits package.

Every radical middle thinker I know would allow, even encourage us to purchase as much private health insurance as our fretful hearts desired. What we'd be required to purchase, though—and what the subsidy might cover or help cover—is a basic minimum benefits package. It's the basic benefits package that would determine how healthy and happy and secure we'd all be.

Obviously, hospital and catastrophic care should be covered. But should preventive care be covered? Alternative care? Public health measures? Answer: all of the above. The radical middle is committed to creative public policies and maximizing everybody's choices.

Imagine the kind of health care world that might result. A world in which "client-centered" practitioners would routinely screen kids for depression—women for breast cancer—men for prostate cancer. A world in which you could go to a chiropractor or an acupuncturist or an herbal therapist any time you wanted. A world in which you knew your government was making sure your community water supply was as healthy as could be.

Who wouldn't want to live there?

What's stopping us now isn't cost. To achieve universal health insurance coverage today, the total gross cost would be the number of uninsured (roughly 40 million) times the per-capita cost of coverage (roughly $3,200), or approximately $128 billion per year. Sounds formidable. But according to Danzon and Pauly, the uninsured already consume on average about 60 percent as much medical care as the insured. So additional medical care for the uninsured would cost approximately $51 billion per year.

Far less than we'd save by building in preventive, alternative, and public-health-oriented care, as you'll see below.

MAKE IT PREVENTIVE

Quietly but decisively over the last ten years, physicians and research scientists have proved beyond a shadow of a doubt that many preventive health care measures are effective. I'm not talking about dissident health workers in marginal settings. I'm talking about people—often idealistic Baby Boomers—who worked their way into the heart of the medical profession in order to change it for the better.

Take the physicians and researchers at the U.S. Preventive Services Task Force (USPSTF), an "independent panel" created by the U.S. Department of Health and Human Services. By the early 1990s they had critically assessed the clinical effectiveness of 169 preventive interventions. By 1996 they had zeroed in on approximately 80 health conditions—from "abdominal aortic aneurysm" to "visual impairment"—and recommended preventive interventions (screening tests, counseling, immunizations, etc.) for 30 of them.

Any preventive health care plan worth its salt would mandate or at least offer these interventions. Some examples: vaccinate children against six childhood diseases, provide tobacco cessation counseling, screen adults over 65 for vision impairment, assess dental health practices. A more recent addition to the list: screen adults for depression.

Other champions of preventive care are the physician-researchers at the Centers for Disease Control and Prevention (of the Department of Health and Human Services), "CDC" for short. In its fine report "An Ounce of Prevention—What Are the Returns?," the CDC identified 19 strategies to prevent disease and promote healthy lifestyles. Nine involve screening (e.g., screen women aged 50–69 for breast cancer every one to two years), five involve counseling, three involve immunizations.

The American Academy of Pediatrics is a third crucial player defining basic preventive services. In the year 2000 it released its recommendations for preventive care—a menu of 22 measures to be carried out by health care professionals on (or on behalf of) children from the womb through age 21. The measures range from annual physical exams to a lead screening exam to nutrition counseling.

Stop for a minute. Think how much healthier and happier many of us would be if we'd spent our lives receiving the care called for by the three groups above. A radical middle national health care plan should incorporate into its basic benefits package all the preventive services recommended by all of them.

Not only would we be healthier and happier, in the long run we'd be wealthier. Adding a "core set" of clinical preventive services recommended by USPSTF to private health insurance programs would cost an average of $84 per year for women and $52 for men. Because the radical middle national health insurance plan calls for even more preventive services, let's estimate an average cost of $100 per person per year. That's $28 billion per year.

But wait. Total U.S. health care costs now exceed $1.4 trillion per year. If the $28 billion per year in prevention investments manages to reduce total costs by even 5 percent, they'd go down by $70 billion—saving a cool $42 billion per year. You've heard about doing well by doing good? I call this doing well by *feeling* good.

MAKE IT INTEGRATIVE

If you're of a certain age, chances are good you associate "alternative medicine" with the Sixties counter-culture, and with books that use the word "healing" a lot while brimming with venomous quarter-truths about "Western" science and the medical profession. So you might be surprised to learn that a new breed of alternative health practitioner has come to the fore.

Most of them reject the term "alternative" for the more complex and demanding term "integrative," with its connotations of openness toward all effective conventional and alternative therapies. Even Dr. Andrew Weil, our most prominent popularizer of alternative medicine, prefers the term "integrative" now.

More importantly, most alternative health practitioners want alternative therapies to be tested now—by "Western" scientific methods—as rigorously as other therapies. The National Center for Complementary and Alternative Medicine (NCCAM) has taken the lead here.

Established in 1992 as a mere "Office of Alternative Medicine" (at the National Institutes of Health), and converted into a "National Center" in 1998, its extraordinary team of physician-scientists quickly identified over 600 "complementary and alternative" therapies, and has been testing the most promising of them ever since. Five-year clinical trials are currently underway on, among other things, St. John's wort for depression, shark cartilage for lung cancer, and ginkgo biloba for memory decline and dementia.

If you want to see where NCCAM is heading, read Dr. Kenneth Pelletier's recent book *The Best Alternative Medicine*. Pelletier was the long-time director of the Complementary and Alternative Medicine Program at Stanford Medical School, and his book is the gold standard for books of its type. Drawing on credible scientific research from around the world, it recommends alternative therapies for 76 conditions, from acne to vertigo. The list of therapies is as comprehensive and carefully wrought as the lists of preventive therapies above.

The integrative wing of the alternative medicine movement got a big boost in March 2000, when the White House and Congress created the White House Commission on Complementary and Alternative Medicine Policy. Its 18 members included genuine pioneers like Thomas Chappell (Tom's of Maine, Inc.), Dr. Effie Chow (East West Academy of Healing Arts), and Dr. Dean Ornish. In its final report, issued in the spring of 2002 under the watchful eyes of the Bush Administration, it rather bravely concluded that "any medical or health care intervention that has undergone scientific investigation and has been shown to improve health . . . should be considered for inclusion in health plan coverage."

Even when alternative therapies aren't included in a health plan's basic benefits package, the Commission helpfully added, they can be offered as a special "rider" or "supplement."

A radical middle national health insurance plan should incorporate into its basic benefits package all the alternative therapies recommended by NCCAM, and some of those recommended by Dr. Pelletier. Many of the others recommended by Dr. Pelletier should be made available in a special "rider" or "supplement" for a nominal fee.

If you're afraid all this is some sort of giddy, radical middle "Open, sesame!" that will propel your hypochondriac neighbor to the chiropractor three times a week, well, you're right and you're wrong. He'll go to the chiropractor more, he might even try a magnet healer or two, but he'll probably avoid unnecessary back surgery. So in the long run we'll all be better off financially. (Plus the basic benefits package would surely seek to limit the annual number of visits we could make to the various healers.)

Just think about all the herbal, Oriental, and physical therapies for such traditionally costly conditions as Alzheimer's and cancer, let alone traditional back pain. If alternative medicine allows us to knock even 2 percent off our health care spending, that's $28 billion per year.

MAKE IT PUBLIC HEALTH ORIENTED

It is not enough for a national health care system to be universal, preventive, and integrative. It also has to address the social and behavioral causes of our poor health.

Addressing such so-called soft issues is not soft-hearted. It is eminently radical middle: both practical and future-focused. You can get just as sick from smoking or pollution or failing to exercise as you can from natural causes.

About 40 percent of U.S. deaths are caused by behavior patterns that could be modified by public health interventions—taxes on tobacco, grants to encourage communities to develop great areas for walking and bicycling, etc. But 95 percent of the money we spend as a nation on health each year goes to direct medical care services. Only 5 percent goes to public health.

Two burgeoning organizations want us to change that.

The Partnership for Prevention is one the broadest-based public policy groups in Washington, D.C., with corporations, nonprofits, and state health departments all aboard as members. One of its latest projects was to compile a list of 180 "Prevention Policy Ideas" that includes such practical-and-creative suggestions as:

- Standardize all child safety seats so all seats would fit in all automobiles;
- Fund visitation programs to homes at risk for abuse, neglect, and unintentional injuries;
- Create financial incentives for states to offer increased physical activity in secondary schools;
- Require fast food restaurants to report nutritional information on menus;
- Create special student-loan repayment programs for dentists willing to work in underserved areas or with underserved populations.

Then there's the Office of Disease Prevention and Health Promotion (of the Department of Health and Human Services), which recently brought out its third "Healthy People" document, "Healthy People 2010: Understanding and Improving Health." Heart and soul of the document is an in-depth look at the way public policy can be used to address such supposedly personal troubles as obesity, substance abuse, poor mental health, and irresponsible sexual behavior.

A radical middle health care system can't just focus on providing care to individuals. It must also devote substantial amounts of energy and money to the kinds of public health initiatives trumpeted by the groups above. And before you tell me this will do irreparable harm to the national budget, consider this: even if we quintuple current national expenditures for public health activities, we'd be spending $40 billion per year on them—far less than we'd save by engaging in them.

The U.S. Public Health Service estimates that if we make appropriate public health investments in six areas (heart disease, stroke, occupational injuries, motor-vehicle-related injuries, low birth weight, and gunshot wounds), then within five years health care costs would drop by 11 percent in those areas. Let's conservatively estimate that half of our total health care costs of $1.4 trillion per year are amenable to such savings. That means we'd eventually be saving 11 percent of $700 billion per year—$77 billion per year. Subtracting $40 billion from $77 billion leaves us with net savings of $37 billion per year.

In the end, lack of money is not what's keeping us from being substantially healthier, happier, and more physically and emotionally secure than we are today. Tally all the figures I've provided in this chapter and you'll discover that the radical middle health care plan would save us money—over $50 billion per year.

Capitalism and the private insurance industry aren't the culprits either. Both would flourish alongside a radical middle health care system. Nor does human nature appear to be the culprit—is there any drive stronger than our wanting to be well? The only real culprit appears to be a lack of two prime radical middle qualities: vision and common sense. The radical middle health care plan may be more sensible than the traditional political system can bear.

RESOURCES

Texts

For approaches to universal health coverage using the private insurance system plus government subsidies, see Ted Halstead and Michael Lind, *The Radical Center* (2001), 73–78, and Matthew Miller, "Universal Coverage, American Style," chap. 5 in *The Two Percent Solution* (2003). See also Senator John Breaux, "The Breaux Plan: A Radically Centrist Approach to a New Health Care System," accessible online.

For a sophisticated defense of the additional approaches recommended here, see Pamela Williams-Russo et al., "The Case for More Active Policy Attention to Health Promotion," *Health Affairs Journal* (March-April 2002), accessible online. For admirably pragmatic approaches to preventive health and public health, respectively, see two online booklets by Partnership for Prevention, "Prevention Priorities: A Health Plan's Guide to the Highest Value Preventive Health Services" (2001), and "Nine High-Impact Actions Congress Can Take to Protect and Promote the Nation's Health" (2000).

Groups

National organizations pursuing some or all of the approaches discussed here include American Public Health Association (www.apha.org), Center for Health Transformation (www.healthtransformation.net), Creating Health for All Project of the Institute for Alternative Futures (www.altfu tures.com), Health Priorities Project of the Progressive Policy Institute (www.ppionline.org), Partnership for Prevention (www.prevent.org), and Universal Health Insurance Program of New America Foundation (www. newamerica.net).

5

LAW REFORM AS IF
PEOPLE MATTERED

I WENT TO LAW SCHOOL at mid-career—after nearly three decades as an activist and alternative journalist—in part because I wanted to help open up the legal profession. Many people I knew were taking strong stands on tort reform, the death penalty, and other legal issues, but I was beginning to see things in a radical middle light. As a result, I was becoming less caught up in hot-button issues and more interested in helping the legal profession become a humane environment that offered us a variety of respectful and affordable ways to resolve our disputes. In the summer before law school, I managed to get myself onto the committee setting up the "alternative dispute resolution" section of the American Bar Association, and helped write its first vision statement.

You'd think a law school would have welcomed someone with my interests and priorities. But at many law schools, and especially at the most competitive of them, you quickly discover that issues of process and practice are looked down upon as trivial. If you want to be taken seriously, you've got to channel your energies into extraordinarily abstract defenses of property rights (if you're conservative), free speech over all other considerations (if you're liberal), or criminal defendants' rights (if you're radical)—"big theoretical nondebates," as Harvard's marvelous radical middle law professor Mary Ann Glendon calls them.

In my first year at New York University School of Law, I was taken aside by my very brilliant and accomplished contracts professor and told there was something unbecoming about concerning oneself with "plumbing issues" like jury reform and middle-class access to legal services. Later that year, a female student who'd attended famous private schools her whole life and was deeply committed to criminals' rights referred to my concerns disparagingly as "housekeeping issues."

But I persisted. In my second year, I desperately wanted to take a legal counseling course (that's what lawyers do, right—counsel clients?); but true to form, and unlike Fordham and Cardozo law schools up the street, NYU Law didn't offer one. Our electives included such offerings as Shakespeare and the law, feminist legal theory, and critical race theory. I ended up getting a dean's permission to take the "Introduction to Counseling and Therapy" course in NYU's Graduate Psychology Department, where I was warmly welcomed as some kind of pioneer, being the first law student to take a psych course in anyone's memory.

Unfortunately, prejudice against "housekeeping issues" is not confined to elite law schools. It is reflected in the way the media cover the legal profession—high on politics and courtroom drama, low on what most lawyers and clients actually go through. The media portrait's unreal, but it's sexy and drives ad sales. Even most of the books that appear to be about the legal profession—such as Walter Olson's *The Litigation Explosion* on the right, or Ralph Nader's *No Contest* on the left—turn out, on closer inspection, to consist largely of arguments in favor of shaping the laws, themselves, in a more consistently right- or left-wing direction.

But things aren't always as they seem. If you look below the surface, you'll find that the legal profession is bursting with people and projects that give pride of place to "housekeeping issues." To a new breed of lawyer and legal scholar—to those at the radical middle—issues of legal process and practice are not just important in themselves. They're important because they promise to focus legal reform efforts on a new set of goals—maximizing choices for all participants in the legal system, and making that system as humane as possible. Making it unintimidating for legal consumers, affordable and meaningful for civil litigants, and hands-on and responsive for criminal litigants.

UNINTIMIDATING

One of the easiest ways to make the legal system less intimidating for legal consumers is to put something like a "Legal Consumers' Bill of Rights" into all attorney contracts.

For all the lawyer shows we watch on TV, most of us are at the mercy of our lawyers. Most of us haven't the faintest idea what to do when a lawyer charges us excessive fees, neglects our case, lies to us, or performs incompetently. A legal consumer's bill of rights—which all lawyers would be required to provide their clients—could tell us exactly how to proceed.

Another way to make the legal system less intimidating would be to offer introductory legal education in high schools. Street Law, Inc., has proved it can be done. The D.C.-based organization has been helping U.S. high schools create courses in law for two decades now—it's written a compelling textbook on practical, real-world, "street-level" law, set up law-related education centers in every state, and gotten thousands of law students to lend high school teachers a hand. It's time for the U.S. Department of Education to promote Street Law's programs broadly and systematically.

AFFORDABLE AND MEANINGFUL

Justice is a mirage if you can't afford it. The quest for justice is a lot more pleasant if you can choose among different routes to it. And justice is a lot more meaningful if you can play some role in bringing it about—if you don't just rely on a lawyer to "give" it to you. Those are the reasons radical middle activists support much larger roles for small claims courts and mediation.

Small claims courts are for small claims only. If you want to sue for more than about $2,000 to $5,000 (the max varies by state) you'll have to go to regular court. But small claims courts have some wonderful advantages even today.

Filing, preparing, and presenting a small claim costs next to nothing in most states—often under $50. It is relatively easy (generally there are some brief, self-explanatory forms); most people can handle both the paperwork and the appearance before the small claims judge without a lawyer. And the process is relatively quick: most disputes are heard within a month or two.

I think small claims courts should be dramatically expanded in at least four ways:

- *Raise the monetary ceiling.* I'd raise it from $2,000-$5,000 to at least $25,000. Most people can't afford lawyers to handle disputes much below $25,000. Raise the ceiling to $25,000 and I think you'll see a virtual stampede into small claims courts . . . which may be one reason governments and the legal profession are keeping the ceilings so low.
- *Allow diverse, non-monetary remedies.* In most states, small claims courts can only assess money damages. No radical middle activist—for whom creativity and imagination are prime— should sit still for this. At the very least, judges should be empowered to issue "cease and desist" orders in disputes between neighbors and in contract disputes. Ideally remedies would be limited only by the imagination of the judge and the litigants.
- *Increase people's access.* If more of us had access to small claims courts, more of us would use them! So first and foremost, all small claims courts should hold weekend and evening sessions. In addition, governments should provide better information about local small claims courts—leaflets or brochures in plain English, and websites prominently linked to regular court sites. Radical middle governments would put full-time "small claims advisors" in storefronts or courthouses.
- *Raise the pay for judges.* "The only danger with raising the small claims limits is that we have a shortage of good lawyers who want to be small claims judges," says Ohio appeals court judge Mark Painter. "Unfortunately, the prestige factor is as low as the pay." The greater prominence and bite of small claims courts will deal with the prestige factor, but taxpayers will have to help with the pay.

Mediation is another way to introduce affordability, choice, personal responsibility, and imagination—all key radical middle values—into the legal process.

When I was working for a business litigation firm in Rockefeller Center, I'd often walk home at night haunted by the feeling that nearly every one of our multi-million-dollar clients would have been better off in mediation. One client had been battling his "enemies" (mostly relatives) in court for 13 years; it was the very centerpiece of his existence. I felt our clients needed to be put in settings where they'd be encouraged (or even forced) to face their opponents in a direct and psychologically mature way.

Other legal practitioners shared my feelings, and in 1998, Congress finally passed a law that not only requires all U.S. district courts to devise and implement their own Alternative Dispute Resolution (ADR) programs. The law allows district courts to *force* parties to go to mediation before trial. (Parties aren't forced to accept the outcome of the mediation, though.)

The far right laughed; the far left howled (many leftists are convinced that ADR is a nefarious plot to deny The People their day in court). Many traditional attorneys are up in arms because the ADR law appears to cast some doubt on their all-purpose relevance. But a recent appeals court ruling makes it look like the law will stay. And in districts that aren't overwhelmingly prejudiced against ADR, the law is a huge success, with settlement rates sometimes exceeding 50 percent. Even in litigation-lovin' Washington, D.C., 30–35 percent of the cases referred to the mediation panel are settled there.

Meanwhile, mediators across the U.S. are scrambling to keep up with the demand for their services. Training centers for mediators range from the Harvard-associated Center for Mediation in Law to the International Online Training Program on Intractable Conflict, and mediation courses are taught in virtually every U.S. law school—unimaginable two decades ago. Judicial Arbitration and Mediation Services, now the U.S.'s largest private ADR service (and one of my ex-employers), has developed nine approaches to mediation ranging from the highly structured to the neo-New Age. If that isn't maximizing choices for everyone, then I don't know what is.

HANDS-ON AND RESPONSIVE

About 12 years ago now, I was assaulted by a gang of "troubled youths" a couple of blocks from the big train station in Washington, D.C. I still bear physical and mental scars from the incident, and if I hadn't been going to my aerobics classes faithfully, this book might not be in your hands. Anyway. A couple of days after the incident, I spoke with a policeman across the street from where I'd been attacked. He told me there'd been at least half a dozen attacks in that same spot, and he was pretty sure he knew where most of the culprits were staying. But he didn't see any point trying to catch them, he said (with both sorrow and rage in his eyes). At best, they'd be back on the street three days later, bolder than ever.

The incompetence of our criminal justice system has stuck in my craw ever since. And law school did nothing to help. The arguments in my classes between the civil-liberties-first-second-and-last crowd (about 90 percent of the teachers and students) and the few dissenters (mostly right-wing ideologues) were painful to endure. Neither side seemed to dwell in the real world, where violence and menacing behavior is indeed a real and present danger, but where you can't just put every street punk, mugger, pimp, prostitute, shoplifter, and druggie in jail and throw away the key.

The emerging radical middle solution to the reality of low-level crime is unabashedly down-to-earth. It's to introduce "problem-solving courts" to neighborhoods and communities across the U.S. Problem-solving courts are barely ten years old but have already caught the attention of many of our best criminologists and social scientists. They include drug courts, youth courts, family treatment courts, homeless courts, and general all-purpose neighborhood courts.

Problem-solving courts are—in the best radical middle tradition—both highly pragmatic and highly creative. And they offer criminal suspects an option other than traditional adversarial "justice." If your crime is less than a serious felony, and you're fortunate enough to have an applicable problem-solving court in your community, you can choose to have your case handled there.

But watch out for what you wish for, you might get it.

Problem-solving courts are not soft on crime. One recent study found that the best-known problem-solving court—the Midtown Community Court near Times Square in Manhattan—hands out more and tougher sentences than the downtown court. But defense attorneys and criminal suspects are flocking there regardless. Problem-solving courts provide a unique combination of punishment and help, and everyone knows criminals need both.

At problem-solving courts, offenders are held accountable to neighborhood stakeholders, not just to some abstract idea of goodness. So they're typically sentenced to pay back the community through projects like caring for street trees, removing graffiti, cleaning transportation stops and subway stations, and sorting items for recycling. At the same time, the court links offenders to drug treatment, health care, education, job training, and other social services to help them resolve their life problems.

At Manhattan's state-of-the-art problem-solving court, all these social services can be found on-site. It's extraordinary—it's a one-stop be-accountable-and-rehabilitate-yourself center. Many problem-solving court staffs now include social workers, mediators, victim advocates, job developers, and managers for community service work projects.

If you want to see radical middle creativity at work, look at how roles change in a problem-solving court. Prosecutors and defense lawyers are not only less adversarial—they often work together to ensure that offenders will succeed in their treatment and rehabilitation plans. Judges are not detached, Olympian figures. They'll often question defendants at length, sometimes even dress them down or joke with them, and—most importantly—counsel and dialogue with them.

Even community residents (often crime victims themselves) are part of the picture. They'll sit on problem-solving court advisory boards, help choose and structure offenders' community service projects, and sometimes even meet with offenders.

The traditional left and right have not bought into problem-solving courts, and you can see why. Rigid procedure and zealous advocacy are both giving way to other and more therapeutic objectives. Most defenders of problem-solving courts wouldn't deny that at all. They'd just say it's time we paid more attention to the real-world results of our criminal justice system, and less attention to the formulaic trappings. I couldn't agree more.

Another piece of the radical middle approach to criminal law is as creative as problem-solving courts, and at least as pragmatic—even downright gritty. It's the approach to criminal sentencing known as "restorative justice."

Restorative justice gets us away from the left-right criminal justice dance. Your goal is neither vengeance nor forgiveness. It is to repair (or prevent) as many harms as possible. It is to render the offender accountable, repair the victim, and try to heal offender, victim, and community. That's why it's called "restorative."

In good radical middle fashion, restorative justice gives confessed or convicted criminals a choice. They can either be sentenced by the trial judge or they can be sentenced by the judge in consultation with other relevant parties (assuming those parties approve!).

Some pre-sentencing processes are as simple as a victim-offender mediation. Victims meet their offenders under the watchful eye of a trained mediator, and if all goes well the offender learns about the crime's severe impact and the parties figure out how the offender can best make amends (provide "resti-tution"). Their plan is then presented to the sentencing judge. Already—with minimal state support—over 300 victim-offender mediation programs are hard at work in North America today.

Other pre-sentencing processes can involve many more parties—not just victim, offender, and facilitator, but family, friends, prosecutor, defense counsel, police and court workers, community representatives, and even the judge. With enough participants these groups can't help but remind you of the peacemaking or sentencing circles of traditional Native American practice, and the goal is the same too: to give everyone a voice in coming up with a constructive plan that can lead to reparation and peace.

I think small claims courts, mediation services, problem-solving courts, and restorative justice are building blocks for an entire radical middle judicial philosophy. Some have begun calling it "therapeutic jurisprudence," because its central focus would be the law's impact on the social and psychological well-being of all citizens.

And what could be more needed, now, than that? For those of us at the radical middle, the "majesty of the law" is not its impersonality or finality or intellectual grandeur. It is its awesome capacity to help us run a humane U.S. household.

RESOURCES

Texts

For a consumer-rights approach to law reform, see the HALT website (www.halt.org). For a positive vision of small claims courts, see Ralph Warner, *Everybody's Guide to Small Claims Courts*, 9th ed. (2003), chap. 25. For radical middle approaches to mediation, see Jennifer Beer, *The Mediator's Handbook*, rev. ed. (1997), and Robert Mnookin, *Beyond Winning* (2000).

For an overview of problem-solving courts, see John Feinblatt et al., "Neighborhood Justice: Lessons from the Midtown Community Court" (1998) or Eric Lee, "Community Courts: An Evolving Model" (2000), both accessible online. For radical middle jurisprudence, see Prison Fellowship International, "What Is Restorative Justice?" (2000), and David Wexler, "Therapeutic Jurisprudence: An Overview" (1999), both accessible online. For a brilliant, in-depth look at one type of problem-solving court that also touches on questions of restorative justice and therapeutic jurisprudence, see James Nolan, Jr., *Reinventing Justice: The American Drug Court Movement* (2001).

Groups

Organizations pursuing approaches discussed here include Association for Conflict Resolution (www.acrnet.org), Center for Court Innovation (www.courtinnovation.org), HALT: An Organization of Americans for Legal Reform (www.halt.org), International Centre for Justice and Reconciliation of Prison Fellowship International (www.restorativejustice.org), International Network on Therapeutic Jurisprudence (accessible online), and Section of Dispute Resolution of the American Bar Association (www.abanet.org).

6

HOW TO STOP BEING
DEPENDENT ON OIL

S A YOUNG ACTIVIST AND AUTHOR, I was invited to speak at the Toward Tomorrow Fair in Amherst, Mass., in the summer of 1978. Thousands of people came to the event from all over the world—to this day it's remembered as one of our grandest "alternative energy and appropriate technology" celebrations. The topic of my speech and workshop was Lifestyle Change—The Most Important Way We Can Save on Energy.

I was a passionate and, I must confess, rather self-righteous advocate of "simple living" in those days. That made me a perfect speaker for the Fair. It was a virtual bedlam of competing claims from equally self-righteous proponents of the different energy paths, conservation, solar power, wind power, hydrogen, etc., not to mention "technofixes" of the dominant energy paths (coal, oil, nuclear).

The Toward Tomorrow Fair did portend the future, but not in the way any of us had hoped. Competition—not clarity—reigned supreme in the decades after the Fair, and no energy path rose to a point where it could challenge conventional coal and oil.

Support for nuclear energy waned . . . but so did support for lifestyle change. President Carter's "malaise" speech and cardigan sweaters turned conservation into an enduring symbol of American powerlessness. Solar and wind power rose to the top of the alternative energy heap, then faded when it became clear the technologies weren't ready for prime time and a gaggle of shady alternative-energy businessmen kicked the last vestiges of idealism out of the wind power movement. Now hydrogen is the great post-petroleum hope, hyped not just by radicals like Jeremy Rifkin but by sophisticated techno-capitalists at *Wired* magazine and in the (relatively) progressive oil companies like BP and Shell. The cover of the April 2003 *Wired* blares, "How Hydrogen Power Can Save America."

But at this point, who in their right mind would put all their eggs in one alternative-energy basket? Hang out at the annual meeting of the National Hydrogen Association conference, as I did last year, and along with enthusiasm you'll hear a barrelful of doubts, fears, uncertainties, and "if-onlys"—just as you'll hear at any other energy conference, oil to solar.

PARALLEL ENERGY PATHS

Given this situation of public preening and private uncertainty, the radical middle couldn't be more timely.

On the right, the impulse is to stick with oil and coal by any means necessary. On the left, the impulse is to pick the alternative energy path du jour and pump billions of dollars of government money into "perfecting" the technology. The radical middle says no to both those impulses.

The radical middle is not about picking winners. It is especially not about picking winning energy paths, which truly requires a crystal ball.

The radical middle is about maximizing choices . . . not just for individuals but for government policy makers. And it is—as we've seen—about doing what Ben Franklin did so well, maximizing both pragmatism and creativity.

So the radical middle way to achieve energy independence is to promote *whatever combination* of energy sources, technological changes, and value changes can render us least dependent on oil, with due consideration as to safety and price.

Many caring energy professionals have begun to rethink their natural competitive tendency to promote their energy path at the expense of all other energy paths. For example, Steve Chalk, head of the Hydrogen Program at the Department of Energy, says that "diversification" is what we should be after—developing nuclear, devcloping biomass, developing as many viable alternatives to oil as possible.

Hank Habicht, a commissioner at the recently launched National Commission on Energy Policy, is another hydrogen enthusiast who's wary of putting all our eggs in the hydrogen basket. He preaches a gospel of "hydrogen-and": hydrogen and renewables, hydrogen and conservation, hydrogen and—even—carbon-free coal technology.

Radical middle thinkers want all the players in the post-oil energy fight to commit themselves to listening to one another and learning from one another. That doesn't mean holding hands and singing "Kumbaya" at national energy conferences. It means favoring support—both public and private—for all reasonable research, development, and demonstration projects by every non-oil player, solar to nuclear, hydrogen to natural gas.

Some radical middle energy policy analysts have given a name to this all-inclusive, all-for-one approach: "diverse energy paths" (a takeoff on the narrower, Seventies notion of "soft energy paths"). I prefer the term "parallel energy paths" because it emphasizes the different energy paths' coexistence over time, with some being preferable today, others tomorrow, and so on back and forth into the distant future.

SEVEN PATHS OVER AMERICA

Remaining dependent on oil is no longer an option. We import 55 percent of our oil now, according to *Business Week*—up from about 33 percent in the 1970s. We're more dependent on the good offices of our Middle Eastern "allies" than we've ever been. Saudi Arabia alone has the capacity to make or break world oil prices, a truly unsettling thought given many Saudis' ambivalence toward us even after 9/11.

You might think it's enough for us to liberate ourselves from dependence on foreign oil. But it's not. We need to liberate ourselves from dependence on oil itself. Economists across the political spectrum have concluded that even perfect self-sufficiency in oil can't protect us from price hikes by oil producers. To the extent that oil is a fungible global commodity—pretty much the same no matter where on Earth it's found—oil prices will be roughly the same for us whether we get our oil from the Middle East or East Texas, the Nigerian coast or the Alaskan slope.

What all this means is that we cannot pursue a traditional oil energy path. We have got to get off the oil path pronto. It is not a matter of ideology. It is a matter of protecting our country from oil price shocks and oil price blackmail . . . not to mention climate change and air pollution threats arising from our use of oil.

The radical middle notion of parallel energy paths couldn't be more timely. Using parallel energy paths, we can move away from oil dependence in a thoughtful, balanced, future-focused way. All we need to do is have the government provide support to each of several very different energy paths—and have our society make use of each whenever and to the extent that each promises to meet our energy needs cheaply and safely.

I nominate seven energy-related paths to focus on: conservation, renewables, clean fossil fuels, hydrogen, nuclear, biobased fuels, and values-change. Among them, these paths are diverse—so diverse that neither conservatives, nor liberals, nor radicals would likely support them all. But each path exemplifies radical middle practicality and vision. And each appears to hold real promise for the near- or long-term future:

The conservation path.

Few conservationists still claim that conservation (now often called "energy efficiency") can eliminate most of our energy needs. However, the best of them—such as Howard Geller, until recently director of the American Council for an Energy Efficient Economy—are convinced that adopting a comprehensive set of conservation policies could lower national energy use by up to 20 percent over the next ten years.

Those policies are not difficult to grasp. They could include tax incentives for producers and consumers (for example, a tax credit for builders of energy-efficient homes, and a tax credit for buyers of such homes). They could include strengthening efficiency standards on products like household appliances. And they could include raising miles-per-gallon standards on cars and trucks. The recent East Coast and Midwest power outage drew attention to a policy many of us hadn't thought about: converting our outdated electricity grid into a smart and digitally controlled network.

The renewables path.

Renewable energy should be another permanent part of our nation's energy arsenal. Who knows how cheap and effective these technologies will ultimately be? One thing is clear: the more that wind and solar energy devices are used, the faster the price will come down (because of economies of scale in both production and delivery). So if you want to see renewables take hold, push for their adoption by any means necessary!

Some means are already at hand. Some states are thinking about reducing taxes for renewable energy companies. Others are considering partnering with private companies in the development of renewable energy. A more subtle means is the "production tax credit" (PTC). The federal government now provides a PTC of 1.5 cents per kilowatt-hour to producers of electricity from wind energy. Puny—but it's a start. About a third of the states have adopted something called the "renewables portfolio standard," a boring-sounding name for a wonderful idea: making utilities provide a certain minimum amount of energy in the form of renewables. In New York, for example, utilities are going to have to provide 25 percent of energy from renewable sources by the year 2012.

The fossil fuels path.

It is fashionable in some circles to count fossil fuels out, but I don't share that view. There are many good reasons to move away from oil, as I've explained above. But other fossil fuels can be more than transitional. They can be part of our permanent energy arsenal.

Natural gas, for example, is currently looked down upon as an energy source that's cleaner than oil but intrinsically inferior to renewables. But will it always be so? Some research scientists think that the "combined cycle gas turbine" will—within two decades—produce power from natural gas that's as clean and cheap as we could possibly want. In addition, some industry analysts are convinced that so-called clean coal—coal turned into energy by advanced, emissions-free technology—is on the not-so-distant horizon.

The hydrogen path.

There is every reason to believe that hydrogen will make a powerful contribution to meeting our energy needs. The relevant technology is already at hand: the hydrogen fuel cell. By mixing hydrogen and oxygen, fuel cells generate only two products—water and electricity—and even the water is said to be clean.

So what's stopping us now? First, the cells are phenomenally expensive. Second, we'll have to build a whole new infrastructure to deliver hydrogen to cars and generators. Building the infrastructure will take time and money, but bringing the cost of the cells down is the dicier proposition. There are other research and development issues as well. We'll have to determine the best way to make the hydrogen (a determination that will surely evolve over time). We'll have to develop safe storage of hydrogen in automobile fuel tanks (a task some hydrogen advocates downplay). And we'll have to develop a fuel tank that can power a car a lot more than the current 200 miles.

The nuclear path.

If you want to distinguish alternative energy advocates from radical middle parallel-pathers, all you have to do is look at their different takes on nuclear energy. The former are almost religiously opposed. The latter are agnostic, more interested in assessing ongoing technological breakthroughs than in refighting ancient battles.

Nuclear is already one of the cleanest sources of energy—nuclear reactors produce no air pollution or greenhouse gases. Nuclear's dangers are well-known; what's less well-known is that nuclear safety and efficiency have increased markedly over the last decade. Workers' exposure to radiation is on the decline—so is waste produced per unit of nuclear energy—and production costs (outlays for fuel, operations, and maintenance) are now 1.8 cents per kilowatt-hour, as compared to 3.5 cents for electricity produced from gas. Most important of all, a new generation of nuclear scientists and engineers—not just in the U.S. but around the world (and especially in Asia)—is dedicated to coming up with solutions to the problems associated with nuclear power.

The biobased path.

Probably the least-known energy path is biobased fuel, and that's not surprising. Biobased fuel is neither romantically "natural" like wind or solar nor romantically high-tech like nuclear or hydrogen. In fact, it is a fascinating mix of both elements. It is ethanol—"good old familiar grain alcohol," as author Walter Truett Anderson puts it. But it is produced with the help of genetically-engineered bacteria and crops.

The biotech production method doesn't win biobased fuel many friends in alternative energy circles. But that very method could make it possible for large amounts of alcohol fuel to be produced relatively cheaply from an enormous variety of organic wastes, from cornfield leftovers to wood chips to grass. And that's important, since there's a lot of biomass in the world, and much of it is inedible and unusable as fuel in its natural state.

If biomass processing develops on a large scale in the U.S., it could revitalize the economies of many farm states. If it develops abroad, it could lead to subsistence farmers in Africa and Latin America being paid to grow crops or gather organic wastes for fuel.

The values-change path.

It's as true today as it was in the Seventies: even a small change toward simpler living would cause energy demand to plummet. That's why the values-change path is just as relevant to our energy future as the other paths above.

It's just as much a phenomenon of private and government initiatives, too. People ranging from former Reagan domestic policy analyst Dinesh D'Souza to former Clinton Labor Secretary Robert Reich have called on Americans to rethink their materialistic values. The "What Would Jesus Drive?" campaign, led by the National Council of Churches (NCC), sparked a colorful debate. I'd like to see a national commission set up to publicize the ideas being discussed by D'Souza, Reich, and the NCC. I'd also like to see some radical middle creativity applied to the tax code. How about a "Living Lightly" deduction of $1,000 for anyone with a college degree earning under $24,000 a year? How about similar-sized deductions for heads of auto-free households and heads of households with under three kids?

To sum up: don't let anyone tell you that any of the seven energy-related paths above shouldn't be cultivated to the max. If they do, they're talking ideology, not science or even common-sense. It is simply impossible for any person to know, now, which of the paths will turn out to be better or best . . . or at which point or points in their development.

EVENTUALLY WE'D SAVE MONEY

Estimates are that it will cost $200 billion to carry out our mission in Iraq over the next ten years. That's about as much as it would cost to do something at least as pressing: free ourselves from dependence on oil by adopting the radical middle parallel-paths energy strategy.

What if each year for the next ten years, all seven energy paths received $2.86 billion in grants, tax benefits, and other subsidies? Every path but one (fossil fuels) would receive an immense—and hopefully galvanizing—financial boost. And those in the fossil fuels sector, seeing the writing on the wall, might devote more of their wealth to R&D in clean coal and natural gas technologies.

Is $200 billion reasonable? It is an open secret among energy policy analysts that fossil fuels and nuclear energy receive hidden or inefficient subsidies totaling at least $300 billion per year worldwide. Much of that consists of what economists call externalities—indirect costs that society has to pay when, for example, fossil fuels pollute the air and streams. So even though a ten-year, $200 billion energy budget sounds huge, it needs to be seen in context.

And when you look at the savings we'd get, it begins to look like a smart investment. According to the Tellus Institute, if a broad portfolio of post-petroleum policies and measures were adopted, the net savings would be more than $80 billion a year by 2020.

Since at least the Toward Tomorrow Fair we've had to watch passionate partisans of solar power, nuclear energy, hydrogen fuel cells, etc., toot their own horns while the U.S. became ever more dependent on oil. Many of them saw themselves as heroes. In reality, they were following a self-defeating strategy built on irresponsible visionary promises and the One Right Way. I think it's time to adopt a radical middle strategy built on pragmatism-coupled-with-vision and maximization of policy choices over time.

With oil dependence threatening our future, I think it's time for advocates of all seven promising energy paths to accept—eagerly, even joyously—what each path could conceivably add to the whole. And then to move forward, together.

RESOURCES

Texts

For an accurate statement of the problem, see Ronald Minsk, "Ending Oil Dependence as We Know It," Progressive Policy Institute (2002), accessible online. For a useful thought experiment, see Shell International, "Energy Needs, Choices and Possibilities: Scenarios to 2050," accessible online. For a bittersweet look at what happens when alternative technologies are marketed too early, see Peter Asmus, *Reaping the Wind* (2001).

For passionate but also thoughtful and sensible approaches to each of the parallel energy paths, see Alliance to Save Energy et al., "Increasing America's Fuel Economy" (2002), accessible online; National Renewable Energy Laboratory's website (www.nrel.gov); Energy Research Centre's "Clean Fossil Fuels" website (www.ecn.nl/sf); Robert Rose, "Fuel Cells and Hydrogen: The Path Forward," Breakthrough Technologies Institute (2002), accessible online; Richard Rhodes and Denis Beller, "The Need for Nuclear Power," *Foreign Affairs* (January-February 2000); Walter Truett Anderson, "Moving Toward a Biobased World," Pacific News Service (2000), accessible online; and—for the values change path—the Co-op America website (www.coopamerica.org).

Groups

National organizations that appear to be taking moderately if not maximally collaborative approaches to our energy future include American Council on Renewable Energy (www.americanrenewables.org), Electric Power Research Institute (www.epri.com), Fostering Sustainability Project of the Institute for Alternative Futures (www.altfutures.com), National Commission on Energy Policy (www.energycommission.org), and National Energy Policy Initiative (www.nepinitiative.org).

PART THREE

GIVE EVERYONE
A FAIR START

7

GREAT TEACHERS, GREAT TEACHERS, GREAT TEACHERS

IN MANY WAYS I ENVY my adopted nephew, Christopher. Though he's barely eight, he's quick-witted and sassy, has extraordinary physical ability, great musical ability, and tremendous insight into people's character. When I carried him (a stringy black kid from Oakland) on my shoulders through the Denver zoo, he understood immediately that people were staring at us out of curiosity not hostility. It took me about four decades to develop so generous a heart.

So I was stunned the other day when my sister called from Oakland and, during a lull in the conversation, let me know that Chris had failed first grade.

I couldn't believe it. With his sharp intelligence and fine sensibility, my fear was he'd be bored in class—not that he'd feel intimidated or overburdened. But there it was.

My sister told me he'd ended up with a poor teacher. Didn't bond well with Chris. Didn't seem to take much interest in him, couldn't get much work out of him. But his next teacher would be better, my sister (a good Democrat) quickly added.

I was polite on the phone. But inside, I was seething. No teacher should be in a classroom if he or she can't stimulate someone as naturally quick and wise as Chris. And to be honest, I was just as angry at my sister. How could she be so nonchalant about what had happened to Chris? Didn't she know—as I knew—that Chris was plenty bright enough to pick up on the negative messages his "teacher" had just sent him?

In this, my sister seemed no different from many other Americans who passively accept the mediocre to incompetent educations their kids receive in the inner cities, and elsewhere as well. For sure, many K–12 teachers are doing a creditable job (particularly outside the urban environment); all teachers are underappreciated; most are grossly underpaid. But I cannot, for the life of me, understand why urban Americans aren't streaming out into the streets demonstrating—even rioting—against what's being done to their sons and daughters in the public schools. It's their very futures, and ours, that are at stake.

At the radical middle, fixing America's public schools is a dominant concern. One of our key value commitments is providing a fair start in life for everyone. That can't happen if our biggest school systems don't teach real well. Also, most of us are knowledge workers, and we understand better than traditional liberals and radicals that the 21st century—brimming with awesome science and technology, and awash in depthful artistic and social-scientific expression—belongs to the well-educated. Our response to that is to try to educate everyone well . . . not to wax romantic about industrial jobs and bowling leagues.

I suspect one reason Americans of all races and social classes are not in the streets is we don't realize the magnitude of the problem. Urban public education is not a sexy issue for the media, and most newspaper stories I've seen on the subject are a bit sugar-coated, to say the least. Anyone who wonders why we're bifurcating into a two-tier society should sink their teeth into facts like these:

- Over the last 30 years, per-pupil expenditures on public K–12 education after adjusting for inflation have more than doubled. Nevertheless:
- International tests of students from developed countries continue to show U.S. high school students ranking near the bottom in mathematics and science;
- Over 30 percent of U.S. college freshmen now need remedial courses in reading, writing, or math after arriving on campus;
- Only 7 percent of U.S. 17-year-olds can now read and understand "specialized materials," and only 2 percent—2 percent!—can write logical, focused prose.

Despite this miserable state of affairs, our politicians have failed to propose solutions that go to the heart of the matter. Instead, they're offering up their favorite magic bullets.

On the right, the solution is said to be "raising standards"—i.e., turning schools into little factories for raising scores on standardized tests. Does that sound like what education's supposed to be about to you?

On the left, the solution is said to be reducing class size. But why should schools that are doing a dismal job with 25–30 kids per class, suddenly become competent and inspiring with 20–25 kids per class? Many European countries average over 30 pupils per class, and Switzerland averages close to 40.

Maybe high-stakes testing will frighten some students into memorizing more names and dates. And it couldn't hurt if classes were smaller (though credible studies find class size has no significant impact beyond K–3). But no political leader in this country—of any party—has the courage to stand up to the education bureaucracy and say what's become obvious to the American people as a whole and to a rapidly growing galaxy of "radical middle" education researchers and reformers:

The teacher is the key to reinventing American education.

Our schools don't need more high-stakes testing, stricter graduation requirements, smaller classes, more computer-driven learning, or prettier buildings, nearly so much as they need the one thing money and power alone can't generate: Great teachers.

THE PEOPLE SPEAK

That may be heresy to the folks at the Department of Education and the teachers' unions, but it's common sense to the American people.

When Daniel Yankelovich's Public Agenda polling firm asked, "What is the most important thing public schools need in order to help students learn?," the most common response—by far—was, "Good teachers."

And in a poll conducted for the report *The Essential Profession* (2001), when Americans were asked how to improve student learning, "Ensuring a well-qualified teacher in every classroom" ranked second at 89 percent—only one percentage point below "Schools safe from violence."

Third was "Greater parental involvement" (86 percent), fourth "Getting fully qualified principals" (84 percent), fifth "A challenging curriculum" (75 percent). All inextricably linked to landing and retaining great teachers.

The magic bullets of the left and right brought up the rear: tenth was greater access to computers (64 percent), 11th was reduced class size (60 percent), 12th was public school choice (47 percent), and 13th was promoting students based on standardized test scores (28 percent).

Most education experts are happy to defend the officially sanctioned magic bullets. But experts at the radical middle have begun giving voice to what the American people already know: teachers are the key. Former public school and Harvard University teacher Peter Temes puts it succinctly: "What matters most is what teachers do and say with their students." California high school teacher and education workshop leader Brian Crosby is equally blunt: "For too long, education reformers have overlooked—or refused to believe—that the quality of the instructors matters most."

At the heart of the "great teacher" solution to our floundering urban schools is producing a new teaching *culture*—a truly professional and humane culture comparable to that of other professions at their best.

No talented person wants to work in a culture that's characterized by mediocrity, bureaucracy, and conformity—and, unfortunately, too many school systems reek of all three. According to one study, the average SAT score for ed majors is an alarmingly low 964 (the U.S. median is 1,026; the Iowa State University median, 1,210). And staggering numbers of teachers flunk "teacher competency" tests whenever states have the courage to administer them in the teeth of opposition from the teachers' unions. In Massachusetts, 59 percent of teachers flunked the first state competency test.

The U.S. Department of Education reports that half of all new teachers quit, voluntarily, within five years. But wait, it gets worse: teachers with high test scores are less likely to stay than teachers with lower scores.

Teaching pays poorly, and radical middle activists would change that. But pay isn't the main thing that motivates great teachers, just as it isn't the main thing that motivates other caring people (see Chapter Two). When the polling firm Public Agenda asked beginning K–12 teachers to choose between two schools, one that paid a "significantly higher salary" and one where "administrators gave strong backing and support to teachers," an overwhelming 82 percent chose the latter.

If you pay close attention to what radical middle educators are saying, you can put together a coherent program for building a healthy teacher culture. The first eight points below relate directly to the care and feeding of great teachers. The final four relate to the context.

CARE AND FEEDING OF TEACHERS

Revitalized ed schools.

If you've been to college, you probably remember that the school of education on your campus wasn't taken seriously. Well, little has changed. According to education writer Rita Kramer, "The aim is not to produce individuals capable of effort and mastery, but to make sure everyone gets a passing grade."

The radical middle would insist on making ed schools more challenging. Lawyers have to pass a tortuous bar exam; doctors have to complete difficult internships. Why not give teachers better training?

At the very least, ed schools should require students to master, really master, the subjects they intend to teach. Ed schools should require students to engage in extensive, hands-on student teaching (now more the exception than the rule). And ed schools should require students to learn to relate to a wide variety of children and teenagers, including gifted kids, troubled kids, and kids from minority backgrounds.

Alternative paths to teaching.

Even if ed schools are revitalized (no small task), many radical middle educators are convinced that alternative paths to teacher training should be provided—in part as a way to lure caring and creative spirits to K–12 teaching. Basically, two alternative paths have been suggested, which I call the "broad" and "third" paths.

The broad path, touted by the Fordham Foundation, is wary of all government-mandated approaches to teacher quality. "There is no 'one best system' for preparing and licensing quality teachers," says one recent Fordham manifesto. Principal spokesperson for the third path is Frederick Hess, professor of education at the University of Virginia. Hess is critical of Fordham's perspective, saying it comes dangerously close to suggesting that any smart and talented adult is ready to be an effective teacher. He'd prefer that all teachers meet three formal (but hardly bureaucratic) requirements: hold a college degree, pass a skills and knowledge test, and pass a criminal background check.

Rigorous licensing tests.
Today, ten states will hand out a teachers' license if you've managed to stay awake in your ed school courses. Of the 40 states requiring passage of a test, fewer than half go beyond multiple-choice questions to include an essay.

And you should see those tests. Some unions and civil rights groups oppose rigorous licensing tests; as a result, math questions *for high school teachers* are now at the ninth grade level, and reading passages for teachers are at the level of popular magazines.

Radical middle educators would end this farce. "All candidates should pass . . . rigorous . . . tests of subject matter knowledge and knowledge about teaching and learning before they receive an *initial* license and are hired," says Stanford education school professor and former public school teacher Linda Darling-Hammond. "They should then pass a performance assessment of teaching skills during [a one- or two-year apprenticeship] as the basis for a continuing license."

And apprenticeships for all.
Radical middle educators would not just plunk beginning teachers into the classroom. "The first year or two of teaching should be structured much like a residency in medicine," says Darling-Hammond, "with teachers continually consulting a seasoned veteran in their teaching field about the decisions they are making, and receiving ongoing advice and evaluation."

Career-long development.

Teacher training wouldn't stop after the first couple of years. Lawyers have their "continuing legal education" programs; just so, radical middle educators envision continuing teacher education programs.

Professional development today, says educator-author Peter Temes, is unplanned, uncoordinated, overpriced, and typically provided by jaded consultants who "deliver more or less the same presentation to widely different groups of teachers." Radical middle educators want to see the following:

- school-based research projects, study groups, and peer coaching;
- networks and projects that would allow teachers to work together across schools (or regionally or nationally);
- local or regional "teacher academies" where teachers could go for skill building and problem solving.

Real evaluations.

Most professionals continually seek (or are at least forced to experience) evaluations of their work by their peers. But K–12 teachers have often resisted attempts to evaluate their work. And students have paid the price.

Radical middle educators want teachers to have their work evaluated at periodic intervals. Many point enthusiastically to the National Board for Professional Teaching Standards (much loathed by unions). The Board encourages teachers to submit videotapes of their teaching, lesson plans, and other samples of their own and their students' work. Later, teachers meet with Board representatives to critically review that material; and if they do well, they receive Board certification. Many caring teachers say they trust the Board's evaluations because it's a professional body, not some bureaucracy or the nosy teacher next door giving an opinion on the fly.

No more sinecures.

Radical middle educators are unwilling to defend inadequate teachers, as many teachers' unions do. They understand that if we want good schools populated by great teachers, then not only do the sexual predators have to go; the incompetent have to go. They cripple students' capacity to learn, threaten the future of kids like my nephew Christopher, and help drive talented and sensitive teachers out of the profession.

Part of this can be dealt with by refusing to license poor teachers at the end of their apprenticeship periods. However, part of it is going to have to be dealt with by tough-minded principals and their staffs—and the unions are going to have to be made to cooperate. Perhaps the government could offer to guarantee job retraining for K–12 teachers who can't make the grade.

Professional pay scale.
If K–12 teachers are going to attend challenging, truly professional ed schools, work as diligently as doctors or lawyers for their licenses, undergo demanding apprenticeships, subject themselves to vigorous evaluations, and risk being fired for incompetence at any point in their careers—then they should be paid like professionals, too.

Today, teachers are paid according to how many degrees they hold and how many years they've worked—period. Merit doesn't enter into it. Even demonstrated effort doesn't enter into it. You can see why caring teachers might feel unappreciated, and other teachers might feel unmotivated.

Radical middle educators would base pay raises in significant part on teacher performance. Here are some things teachers could do to increase their pay:

- boost student learning in their classrooms. Or belong to a faculty that boosted learning in its school;
- boost student enthusiasm in their classrooms;
- teach math or science;
- teach in an inner-city school or in a remote rural school district;
- earn certification from the National Board for Professional Teaching Standards (see above);
- work "after hours" with students or at pressing school tasks.

You can see what radical middle educators are driving at here: using pay to induce great teaching. Putting socially responsible capitalism to work in the teaching profession.

It's almost too heretical to contemplate.

CARE AND FEEDING OF CONTEXT
Equalize school funding.

No caring person—e.g., no one who aspires to be a great teacher—wants to serve in an institution or system that's grossly unfair to the people it serves. And the U.S. educational system is grossly unfair. Some school districts boast more than three and a half times more spending per pupil than others, principally because some school districts are many times richer than others.

For radical middle thinkers and activists, this is no small matter. It may be the most pressing civil rights issue of our time.

Federalize school funding.

To resolve the equity issue, many radical middle policy analysts favor federalizing school funding: ending all state and local government spending on public K–12 education, and having the federal government pick up the entire $350 billion price tag. That wouldn't increase total spending one cent (since all that would change is the funding source)—and the federal government could ensure that expenditures per pupil were the same across school districts (after adjusting for cost of living differences, "special needs," etc.).

Relax union regulations.

Hopefully, the teachers' unions will be so thrilled by the powerful new federal commitment to educational equity above that they'll be willing to abandon their most soul-destroying rules and regulations. If not, radical middle politicians, school administrators, journalists, parents, and others are going to have to force them into it.

Performance-based pay must be introduced immediately. And seniority rules should be abandoned ASAP. Seniority-based hiring and firing means that a teacher's classroom performance is irrelevant in staffing decisions. Nothing could be more damaging to students. "It's a system that puts the needs of adults first," says Joe Nathan, director of the radical-middle-oriented Center for School Change in Minneapolis. And you wonder how he defines "adults."

Unions should also abandon the appalling practice of insisting that—when jobs are at stake—veteran teachers be assigned to subjects they haven't been trained in (rather than letting younger, trained teachers get those jobs). This is also extraordinary cruel to students. Partly as a result, a third of high school math teachers, a quarter of high school English teachers, and a fifth of high school science teachers are teaching without a college major or even a minor in their subjects.

Unions have been and can be a net plus for society, but they need to be reinvented for the 21st century. In education, the old hunkered-down union attitude—don't do anything not in your job description, don't assign any extra unpaid work to yourself, leave your individual initiative at the door, etc.—needs to be destroyed, not only for the kids' sake but for all caring teachers' sake. It's amazing what could come of that (can you spell c-r-e-a-t-i-v-i-t-y?). Instead of school systems spending millions of dollars on simple physical plant repair (such as painting walls and repairing desks), shop class teachers could involve students in massive "learning-by-doing" reconstruction projects. Instead of students suffering through conventional school "breakfasts" and "lunches," teachers of agriculture and home ec could team up to have students grow and prepare healthy foods.

Empower school principals.

Few of the steps above can be taken until school principals are empowered to freely hire, fire, nurture, and reward the teachers and other staff people working under them, and shape the budgets of their schools.

Few principals have anything like that kind of power today—but many radical-middle-oriented principals and school superintendents are fighting for it. For example, the executive directors of the National Association of Secondary School Principals and the National Association of Elementary School Principals recently called on the education establishment to "give principals the autonomy to hire (and fire) their staffs and control their budgets [and] reward staff for strong performance."

WE CAN AFFORD THIS

If we spent education funds more wisely, we wouldn't have to raise one cent for the changes described above.

Barely half of U.S. school system staff, 51.6 percent, are actual teachers. (By contrast, 70 percent of many European school staffs are teachers.) Some of the non-teachers can, frankly, go—and many teachers can be much more intelligently utilized. Decentralizing budgetary and personnel decisions down to the level of the school principal would guarantee such changes.

Federalizing educational expenditures shouldn't boost total costs—and might save on administrative costs. Paying great teachers more and weaker teachers less shouldn't markedly increase total expenditures. And creating a more attractive teacher culture should drastically reduce turnover in the teaching profession, leading to billions of dollars in savings per year.

So far as education is concerned, money is the least of our problems; it's already there. Great teachers are largely not there—but they can be.

RESOURCES

Texts

For roughly similar approaches to the one outlined here, see Brian Crosby, *The $100,000 Teacher* (2002); Linda Darling-Hammond, "What Matters Most: Teaching for America's Future," National Commission on Teaching & America's Future (1996), accessible online; Matthew Miller, "Millionaire Teachers," chap. 6 in *The Two Percent Solution* (2003); Stephanie Soler, "Teacher Quality Is Job One," Progressive Policy Institute (1999), accessible online; and Peter Temes, *Against School Reform (And in Praise of Great Teaching)* (2002).

On credentialing issues, see Frederick Hess, "Tear Down This Wall," Progressive Policy Institute (2001), accessible online, and the "Teacher Preparation and Certification" page of the Teacher Quality Clearinghouse, accessible at www.nctq.org. On pay issues, see Brian Hassel, "Better Pay for Better Teaching," Progressive Policy Institute (2002), accessible online. On school funding issues, see Ted Halstead and Michael Lind, *The Radical Center* (2001), 147-56. On union recalcitrance, see Thomas Toch's cover story "Why Teachers Don't Teach," *U.S. News & World Report* (26 February 1996).

Groups

National organizations supporting many or most of the views here include National Commission on Teaching & America's Future (www.nctaf.org), National Council on Teacher Quality (www.nctq.org), Thomas B. Fordham Foundation (www.edexcellence.net), and 21st Century Schools Project of Progressive Policy Institute (www.ppionline.org).

8

~

AFFIRMATIVE ACTION
FOR THE TRULY
DISADVANTAGED—
OF EVERY RACE

I F I WASN'T RACE-CONSCIOUS before arriving at New York University School of Law, I definitely was after my first couple of months there. It's not that anyone baits you on account of race. It's just the opposite: everyone is too sensitive, too jaded, or too worried (about damaging their future careers) to address in-school racial issues, including—crucially—the issue of racial affirmative action. Everyone knows it's huge in terms of who gets into our law school, who gets financial assistance there, who gets picked for law review. And everyone knows the law school administration does not want you asking difficult questions about its methods. So there's this big, loud elephant galumphing around that everyone just pretends isn't there.

My experience of the race issue at NYU Law wasn't confined to elephants. It was crisscrossed by issues of social and economic status.

Unlike virtually every other NYU Law student, whatever their race, my financial situation was not good. For the last 25 years, I'd lived on an average annual income of under $12,000 (that's what political activism and alternative journalism can do for you). I had no assets and no savings. If I was inclined to identify with any group at all when I arrived at law school, it wasn't with my race or sex or even my age group ("over 40s"). It was with my income group—my "economic class," if you will. And that class was in very scarce supply. There weren't even many people from the kinds of places I'd been raised (Moorhead, Minn., and Wichita Falls, Tex.).

I lived in the law students' dorm, and within my first few days I realized that even the casual clothes my dorm-mates were wearing were nicer than my best clothes. I had no idea what to do; I had no money for clothes. Finally I noticed a barrel full of clothes inside the entrance of our law school library. The library check-out person told me that the barrel was always there. It was meant for donations to "the poor."

I waited till no one was around, then quickly rifled through the barrel. I couldn't believe it. There were Perry Ellis and Calvin Klein shirts in there. There was a Brooks Brothers sport coat. Welcome to the world of my fellow students, I thought. I'd never worn good name brands in my life. Many of the items had been professionally laundered or dry cleaned—so as not to "dis" the poor, I supposed.

I left the library in a daze, and came back ten minutes later with my bulky jacket. When the coast was clear, I quickly stuffed two Perry Ellis shirts and the Brooks Brothers coat inside my own shirt, then zipped up the jacket. Then walked out past the security guard, too nervous to even look at him.

Another law school tale: About that same time, I met with an administrator at Student Aid to go over my whole financial situation. Our school had $3.5 million in grant aid to divide among 1,100 students. I was sure I'd get something.

My confidence increased in the tiny waiting room. The door to the administrator's office was open, and I could hear snatches of his conversation with another incoming student—a tall, attractive black woman who spoke in carefully modulated tones and wore a gorgeous pantsuit. The administrator reassured her that the $10,000 she'd be getting annually "may well be supplemented." He told her to come back in a few weeks and see what he was able to do.

He wasn't able to do anything for me, though. I had to beg him for a small emergency loan to carry me through till the time my first student loan monies would arrive. On my way out, I asked if he had any scholarships specifically for older students.

As a matter of fact, he said, his office had recently been offered $250,000 specifically for the use of older students. But he had decided to reject the money if the donor insisted on the "demographic restriction."

"You mean you don't have scholarships for minorities?" I said, trying not to sound as cynical as I felt.

Age restrictions were beyond the pale, he said. He moved his chair back, indicating our meeting was o-v-e-r.

TOWARD SOCIOECONOMIC DIVERSITY

Let me be clear about what I'm trying to illustrate here.

I support diversity in education. I not only support it, I've worked for it ever since I tutored black sharecroppers' kids in Mississippi in 1965. But the way my law school and other professional schools are trying to bring diversity about may be doing more harm than good. Not only is it turning students—all students, all hues—into cynics who learn to play racial or ethnic "identity games" in order to advance within the system. It's only achieving one kind of diversity—racial diversity. It is ignoring socioeconomic diversity.

Radical middle to higher education establishment: We can achieve both kinds of diversity at once!

One of the radical middle's key value commitments is giving everyone a fair start in life. But you're not doing that if your top schools are open only to people at the top of the socioeconomic pyramid.

Despite NYU Law's much-touted 24 percent minority enrollment, its diversity was only skin deep. I have never—before or since—spent quality time in a less economically or culturally diverse environment.

I admired many of my classmates and professors. But nearly everyone there, white or black, male or female, straight or gay, spoke and thought as if they'd been raised by Mrs. NationalPublicRadio.

In my first year of attendance, NYU Law had 50 students from Penn but none from Pitt; 41 students from Yale and 35 from Harvard, but none from U.Conn. and three from U.Mass.; 32 from the University of California but none from the even larger California

State University system (where my father taught and sister teaches).

And hardly anybody at NYU Law even noticed, or notices, or cares, that huge swaths of the working and middle classes are missing.

When the Supreme Court decided in the summer of 2003 to preserve race-based affirmative action at the University of Michigan's law and undergraduate schools (so long as applicants aren't chosen by a rigid "point" system), university administrators everywhere let out a huge sigh of relief. Their biggest PR challenge—maintaining the appearance of diversity in their ranks—would remain relatively easy. All they'd have to do was continue paying attention to the color of our skins.

And they wouldn't even have to reveal how they were paying attention—that was the beauty of getting rid of the point system. So long as they came up with a passable percentage of racial minorities, the selection process could—and you better believe it, would—remain shrouded in secrecy, just as it was when I attended law school.

Conservatives attacked the Supreme Court decision for refusing to assert that the law is supposed to be color-blind. (No exceptions? Ever?) Liberals cheered the decision, but many of them seemed as irresponsible as the conservatives. Would the Court's decision lock race consciousness, interracial jockeying, and ceremonies of racial woundedness into the American experiment for generations to come? Liberals didn't know; liberals didn't care. All they knew was that the Court's decision made them feel, oh, so benevolent.

Only the radical middle was pragmatic enough and future-focused enough (not to mention courageous enough) to get this issue right. Race-based affirmative action is too narrow to take us where we need to go as a nation. Race-based affirmative action is the name, but economic class discrimination is the game.

And if affirmative action is going to help all of us and not just the elites, then Americans are going to have to defy the elites—and tell them that affirmative action in the American context means boosting talented but financially strapped individuals no matter which racial group they approximate best.

We can still do this.

After all, the Court's decision does not force universities or corporations to adopt race-based affirmative action policies. All it does is tell them they can do so if they choose.

We are still free to find alternative routes to a demographically diverse society. We are still free to make affirmative action serve the truly disadvantaged of every color and ethnicity.

And that's what most of us want.

Poll after poll shows that the American people—in its sensible *and* idealistic wisdom—want affirmative action to help people in need, not people who happen to have a certain skin tone.

In January 2003, for example, *Newsweek* found that Americans opposed preferences for blacks in university admissions by 68 percent to 26 percent, but supported preferences for low-income students of all races by 65 percent to 28 percent.

A month later, the *Los Angeles Times* came up with similar results. It found that Americans opposed the University of Michigan's racial preference plan by 56 percent to 26 percent, but supported preferences for economically disadvantaged students of all races by 59 percent to 31 percent.

We want socioeconomic affirmative action, not race-based affirmative action.

THINKING IT THROUGH

At the radical middle, we haven't just come up with an economic class–based alternative to race-based affirmative action. We've made a rigorous, fact-based case for it and tried to imagine how class-based affirmative action might work in practice. The most persuasive radical middle scholars on the subject—Anthony Carnevale, Stephen Rose, and Richard Kahlenberg—are all associated with the Century Foundation, a Washington, D.C., think tank well known for its careful scholarship on path-breaking subjects.

The key point to be made is this: Although blacks and Hispanics are disproportionately poor, racial affirmative action does little to help poor, working-class, or even middle-class students of color. And it does even less to help poor, working-class, and middle-class students generally. Despite the noble rhetoric surrounding race-based affirmative action, it provides a leg up to the already privileged sons and daughters of upper-middle-class minorities—sometimes at the expense of working-class kids of all races.

The elite universities haughtily deny this, of course (most recently in an amicus brief in the University of Michigan case). But the statistics bear it out. By looking intensely at data from our top-tier colleges (namely, our 146 most selective colleges as defined by *Barron's Compact Guide to Colleges*), Carnevale and Rose show that the representation of poor, working-class, and lower-middle-class students is actually *lower* in them than it would be if grades and test scores were the sole basis for admissions.

In other words: today's opaque, race-based admissions programs are making it harder—not easier—for poor kids to catch a break.

Socioeconomic discrimination at our top-tier colleges is far worse than anyone imagines. According to Carnevale and Rose, students from the top economic half of the U.S. take 90 percent of the available slots. Students from the bottom economic half take 10 percent. Even more egregiously, students from the top economic quartile take 74 percent of the slots; students from the bottom quartile, 3 percent.

In other words: wealthy students are 25 times more likely to be found on top-tier college campuses as are poor students. If that doesn't shock the conscience, I don't know what does.

And listen up, elitists: it doesn't need to be that way. I attended Midwestern State University for a while—a no-prestige school in a then-economically stagnant part of Texas—and I haven't a doubt in my mind that the top 3 to 5 percent of students there could hold their own at the Stanfords or Haverfords or NYU Laws of the world.

I was delighted to discover that Carnevale and Rose back me up on this. After examining SAT scores and other data, they conclude there are more than enough high-performing, low-socioeconomic status students in our high schools to quadruple their representation at our top-tier colleges . . . and those colleges wouldn't miss one academic beat.

The real challenge is designing economic class–based affirmative action programs that not only let in significantly more low-status students, but do so without lowering the percentage of "underrepresented" minorities (African Americans, Hispanics, Native Americans) now in our top-tier schools.

A bit of radical middle cleverness, though, is all that's needed. Carnevale and Rose have concocted a plan that would boost representation of the bottom economic half of the population from 10 percent to 38 percent at our top-tier colleges—a giant step for true diversity—and the percentage of underrepresented minorities would decline only slightly, from 12 percent to 10 percent.

I appreciate Carnevale and Rose's pioneering work. But any step backward in minority representation is unacceptable at the radical middle. One of our value commitments, you'll recall, is giving everyone a fair start. And with the U.S. population of blacks, Hispanics, and Native Americans exceeding 25 percent today, even a small reduction in their representation at our top-tier colleges seems brutally unfair (even if you concede, as I do, that attending one of our less selective colleges—and working hard there—can also get you into the halls of power).

Carnevale and Rose fall short by having their admissions officers look at too few factors. As we've seen, the radical middle is concerned with maximizing people's choices and maximizing human potential—with the whole person—not just grades, SAT scores, and economic status. Richard Kahlenberg, who's also published by the Century Foundation, is precisely on our wavelength. He'd have college admissions officers look at student academic performance in the light of seven factors—parental income; parental occupation(s); parental education; family structure (e.g., single parent household?); wealth or net worth (arguably more significant than income); neighborhood poverty rate; and high school poverty rate.

Admittedly, that's a lot of factors. But the task is less daunting than it seems. All the factors are quantifiable—not one of them calls for a subjective judgment (let alone one requiring race discrimination or reverse discrimination). And all the pertinent information is already available to college financial aid officers—either when students provide detailed financial data to qualify for financial aid, or, with regard to the last two factors, through published socioeconomic surveys.

These factors should not only produce the same percentage of minority students we have in our top schools now (while letting in as many bottom-economic-half students as Carnevale and Rose would).

They should also produce more meritorious student bodies in our top schools. A working-class student who earns a GPA of 3.8 and an SAT score of 1250 has almost surely accomplished more than an upper-class student with the same stats.

And who knows what wondrous things might happen at NYU Law School if professors had to explain themselves not only to minorities from Penn and UC-Berkeley, but to bright working-class kids from Pitt and Cal State-Fresno?

POSTETHNICS YES, MULTICULTURALISTS NO

Part of giving people a fair start is getting them into universities that match their talents and capacities. A related part is harder to describe, but no less important. By the time we get to university, we should be seen as—and allowed to be—the complex, multidimensional people we are. We shouldn't be put into boxes based on our racial and ethnic identities.

A huge fight is taking place over this issue just below the surface of events. It pits the radical middle against the combined forces of the left and right. Let's call the radical middle approach "postethnic" and the left-right approach "multicultural."

In the multicultural approach, a person's racial or ethnic identity is prime. You can see why this approach is favored by the hard left, which dreams of coming to power by putting together a coalition of aggrieved groups. It's also favored by the corporate right, which appreciates that institutions tend to be stable when people identify with distinct groups that each get their fair share of the spoils.

The plus side of the multicultural approach is it gives individuals a prefabricated sense of identity and community. No need for messy and time-consuming identity quests, etc. The minus side is that it encourages ethnic and racial rivalries and diminution of the national community.

The postethnic approach is favored by the radical middle. It looks forward to the diminution of group differences and the rise of a new American persona—neither "white" nor "minority"—with a new, blended consciousness (and skin tone).

The postethnic approach is all about the merging of appealing "black" and "white" cultural traits, not to mention the traits of many other racial, ethnic, experiential, etc., cultures and subcultures. It welcomes that merging, seeks in every way to foster it.

The postethnic approach differs from the multicultural approach in another way too: it doesn't see race as the principal barrier to achievement in 21st-century America. It tends to look to such barriers as alienation, resentment, poverty, and lack of self-esteem.

I suspect that the postethnic approach may someday be seen as the essential Hispanic contribution to the radical middle. Gregory Rodriguez, a Gen-X writer at the New America Foundation, reminds us that—unlike English-speaking settlers—Spanish settlers "were willing everywhere they went to allow racial and cultural mixing to blur the lines between themselves and the natives."

At UC-Berkeley, Professor David Hollinger has established himself as a thoughtful spokesperson for the postethnic approach. He makes the point (vital to radical middle activists, who yearn to maximize choice for everyone) that our horizons shouldn't be limited by the descent-defined communities we belong to. He notes that most of us have multiple affiliations—e.g., American, female, Gen-Xer, white, Christian, copyeditor, Microsoft employee, Seattle resident, Democrat—and that most of those are largely up to us. He goes so far as to argue that even ethno-racial affiliations should be "subject to reasonable consent."

But the most persuasive single proponent of the postethnic approach may be social critic Stanley Crouch. "As people of the Americas," he says, "we rise up from a gumbo in which, after a certain time, it is sometimes very difficult to tell one ingredient from another. All of those ingredients, however, give a more delectable taste to the brew."

What Crouch's "gumbo" is, of course, is racial integration, radical middle style—economic, cultural, psychological, moral, and physical. The beginning of the rise of the new American, a product of all the world's races and cultures.

Economic-based affirmative action has the potential to create a thicker and more complex "gumbo" in our top-tier colleges than race-based affirmative action. That's another reason those of us at the radical middle favor it.

RESOURCES

Texts

For the radical middle position on affirmative action, see especially Richard Kahlenberg, "Economic Affirmative Action in College Admissions," Century Foundation (2003), accessible online. See also Kahlenberg, *The Remedy: Class, Race, and Affirmative Action* (1996). For a data-rich survey that concludes low-income students could and should benefit from affirmative action, see Anthony Carnevale and Stephen Rose, "Socioeconomic Status, Race/Ethnicity, and Selective College Admissions," Century Foundation (2003), accessible online. For an extended meditation on why the goals of race-based affirmative action are best pursued by race-neutral methods, see Ted Halstead and Michael Lind, *The Radical Center* (2001), 169–76.

For the radical middle alternative to multiculturalism, see especially David Hollinger, *Postethnic America: Beyond Multiculturalism* (rev. 2000). But see also Christopher Clausen, *Faded Mosaic: The Emergence of Post-Cultural America* (2000); Stanley Crouch, *The All-American Skin Game, or, the Decoy of Race* (1995); Randall Kennedy, *Interracial Intimacies* (2003); Gregory Rodriguez, "Mongrel America," *Atlantic Monthly* (January-February 2003); Richard Rodriguez, *Brown: The Last Discovery of America* (2002); and Stephan Talty, *Mulatto America* (2003).

Groups

The Century Foundation (www.tcf.org) is *the* economic affirmative action think tank. The Diversity Within Unity Platform Project of the Communitarian Network (www.gwu.edu/~ccps) dovetails with the postethnic views expressed here.

9

JOBS FOR EVERYONE.
A FINANCIAL NEST EGG
FOR EVERYONE, TOO

I WAS THE ORIGINAL soft-hearted radical. As a civil rights worker for the Student Nonviolent Coordinating Committee (SNCC) in 1964–65 in Holly Springs, Mississippi, I gave so much of our food away to local black folks that the key black men on our project eventually confronted me and demanded that I stop. "Let the NAA[CP] give 'em handouts!" one of them shouted. Even after that embarrassment I tended toward soft-hearted guaranteed-annual-income plans and "universal capitalism" schemes (giving every family an interest in a sort of government-created mutual fund). Tough-minded conservatism was anathema to me.

Today I'm at the radical middle on the issue of the importance of earning one's keep. If power corrupts, dependency corrupts absolutely; everyone should have to provide for themselves. However, one of the radical middle values is giving everyone a fair start—not to mention a fair middle passage. So it's important to make sure that everyone has access to a job. It's equally important that everyone has access to the financial means—when they reach 18—to choose the kind of work they'll want to do. Everyone should have enough money to attend a public, in-state college, take vocational training, launch a small business, or buy a start-up home.

What turned me around and brought me to the radical middle on the issue of the importance of earning one's keep wasn't just being attacked by a street gang of young, unemployed men (though that helped). It was an extraordinary sociological study conducted from 1968 to 1978 by the U.S. Department of Health, Education, and Welfare, sometimes known as the "negative income tax experiment" or just "SIME-DIME."

In cities across the U.S., some groups of low-income people were told that for a number of years they'd have a floor put under their incomes. Other, similar groups were "control groups" and received no guaranteed incomes. Many liberals and radicals expected that the folks receiving guaranteed incomes would fare better than the control groups. But just the opposite happened. The guaranteed income encouraged people to stop working—not just at first, but in increasing percentages as the years went by. The guaranteed income somehow encouraged poor people to have more children. And instead of stabilizing families, it triggered more separations and divorces.

There's something else that bothers me, now, about the far left's wish that we be given money for free, without working for it. It's the implicit contempt for work. Socialists have gotten a lot of mileage out of stressing the alienation and meaninglessness of most work. But work has a largely positive dimension that we neglect at our peril.

Work is an important way of giving structure and meaning to our lives. It gives us a sense of belonging to our community and of contributing to our country. It serves as a source of upward mobility. And it's what we do to produce much of what we value. Immigrants to the U.S. tend to be astonished both at how hard we work and at how many different goods and services are available to ordinary people. Hey, there's a connection!

At the radical middle, we've come up with three proposals for ensuring that every American can have a decent working life—provide public-sector jobs for all, provide subsidies to employers for creating extra jobs, and provide a "nest egg" of capital at birth so every American can freely decide what they want to do when they reach adulthood.

PUBLIC-SECTOR JOBS

Every American should have access to a job. And one way of guaranteeing that is by providing public-sector jobs to all unemployed Americans.

The idea is beginning to garner support beyond the usual leftist circles. The National Jobs for All Coalition, which is pushing the idea, has added two former Labor Secretaries, a Congressman, and a CEO to its advisory board. Two radical middle-oriented professional organizations—the American Public Health Association and the National Association of Social Workers—have endorsed the idea.

Not only are many Americans unemployed now, many jobs need to get done—real jobs. Construction workers are needed for our crumbling roads and bridges; supervisors are needed for teen recreation programs; teachers' aides are needed for classrooms. The federal government should provide them.

It isn't true that a public jobs program would be fabulously expensive. If done right, it could nearly pay for itself. According to law professor Philip Harvey, a full-fledged program—one that would truly provide jobs for all unemployed Americans—might cost $225 billion a year. That's a lot of money. But the cost could be largely offset.

Twenty percent of it could be recouped through increased income tax and Social Security payments by program participants. Another 60 percent could be covered by funds otherwise spent on unemployment compensation and means-tested income assistance. And the remaining 20 percent could be at least partly recouped through sales of goods and services produced by program participants.

EMPLOYER SUBSIDIES

Some radical middle activists (including yours truly) would rather not see government become the employer of last resort. We think the goal—making sure that everyone who wants to work can do so—can be much more happily and efficiently met by having the government subsidize private employers to hire more workers.

This is such a radical middle idea, drawing equally on government and business, that it's just getting off the ground. Its leading spokespeople are a pair of eminent economists, Edmund Phelps at Columbia and Robert Haveman at Wisconsin.

Phelps has done celebrated theoretical work on the concept of unemployment. But rather than waste his old age gathering accolades, he launched a new project in the mid–1990s, aptly summed up by the title of his book *Rewarding Work*.

Basically, he wants the government to subsidize firms for every low-wage worker they employ—and he wants part of that subsidy to go to the worker. With a subsidy, firms would hire more workers, and the workers they'd hire would be better rewarded. To discourage cheating, he'd have the subsidy take the form of tax credits against the firm's payroll tax or corporate income tax.

His rationale is pure radical middle, part of the effort not to overturn capitalism but to reinvent it by infusing it with social responsibility. Capitalists can only afford to pay workers for their private productivity, he says—their productivity within the business. But government has an interest in seeing work rewarded according to its social productivity: everyone benefits when all citizens can support themselves and be responsible parents and community members.

Haveman would also subsidize low-skilled workers, and he gets admirably specific. For example, he'd have the government provide a tax credit of $5,000 per extra worker to any firm hiring more workers than it did the year before.

That's very smart. Because the subsidy would be a higher percentage of the wages of low-skilled, low-income workers than it would be of the wages of higher-skilled, higher-wage workers, Haveman's scheme would give firms incentive to hire low-skilled workers. "By directly expanding the demand for low-wage workers," he says, "this program would contribute to a reduction of poverty and unemployment."

Because Phelps's and Haveman's ideas can't be reduced to slogans on placards, they lack the sex appeal of "Guaranteed Incomes for All!" or "We Demand a Living Wage!" But if our goal is to create a world where everyone who wants to work will feel invited in and respected, then the subtle and circumspect route those economists propose may be the wiser course.

STAKEHOLDER ACCOUNTS

It is not enough to provide jobs for all. In a truly fair society, we should also want to give everyone an opportunity to prepare themselves for the jobs or futures they'd most like to pursue.

It is not enough simply to inculcate the right attitudes; money is also important. I spent many years in the New Age movement, long enough to know that some of our most prominent proponents of "taking charge of your life," "personal empowerment," and the "psychology of getting ahead" just happen to be recipients of six- or seven-figure trust funds. Something they rarely mention in their books and lectures.

One key to a fair society, then, is figuring out how every single one of us can start off with some kind of nest egg. Not a huge trust fund, of course—but enough to ensure a decent college education. Or, if you're forgoing college, enough to start a small business. Or, if you're intent on starting a family, enough to purchase a small home. Some of us like to call that nest egg a "stakeholder account," for the obvious reason that it gives the holder a stake in the larger society.

Many radical middle thinkers have been devoting themselves to this project, beginning with Michael Sherraden in the early 1990s. Sherraden is head of the Center for Social Development at Washington University in St. Louis. His thesis is that, if you want to encourage people to do well in life, you'll emphasize savings rather than income.

It's common sense, once you think about it. "When people are accumulating assets," Sherraden says, "they think and behave differently and the world responds to them differently as well. Assets improve household stability [and] psychologically connect people with a viable, hopeful future."

Sherraden's main proposal—and it's been experimented with (on a very small scale) in communities across the U.S.—is for the government to set up Individual Development Accounts (IDAs) as early as birth either for poor individuals or all individuals. Every time you deposit money in the account (up to a certain set limit per year), the government or some private sector entity matches your deposit. Maybe the government or private entity even makes an initial deposit on its own, to get the ball rolling.

But you don't get to draw on the account whenever you like. That's the real key. Withdrawals would be restricted to legitimate long-term goals—postsecondary education, home buying, and the like.

Because everyone would have this extraordinary nest egg accumulating from childhood, everyone would grow up feeling like they had a stake in society. "Young people would be given specific information about their IDAs from a very early age," Sherraden says, "and would begin planning for use of the accounts in the years ahead." Schools could teach kids about how to invest their money wisely—a great way to introduce them to subjects like economics and financial planning.

Sherraden's proposal is radical middle to the core. It combines common sense with vision, and helps everyone get a fair start in life. My only concern is that some versions of Sherraden's IDAs might not be large enough to do much good. My sense is that, if you won't be getting a minimum of $20,000 at the age of 18, you're not going to devote a good part of your youth to thinking constructively about how to use the money to launch your career.

Other radical middle thinkers share my concern, and some of us have gone public with more generous asset-building proposals. Three are especially well mapped out:

- Economist Robert Kuttner would give every American child $5,000 at birth. The money would be administered by Social Security and invested in bonds and stock index funds. For low-income children, the government would add $1,000 each year. Middle-income families would get a tax deduction for contributions of up to $1,000 per child per year.

  Half the accumulated money could be spent on college tuition. At age 30, two-thirds of the residue could be spent on home ownership or lifelong learning or job training, and at age 60 the remainder could be used for retirement. The cost— $50–75 billion a year—would be paid for partly by lifting the cap on the income subject to the Social Security tax, and partly by a surtax on big incomes and estates.

- Ray Boshara, director of the Asset Building Program at the New America Foundation (a radical centrist think tank in Washington, D.C.), wants every baby born in America to receive a one-time "endowment" of $6,000. If invested in a relatively safe portfolio with a 7 percent annual return, the sum could grow to more than $20,000 by the time the child reaches 18, and $45,000 by the time he or she reaches 30.

The account would be restricted to such uses as paying for the cost of higher education or vocational training, buying a first home, starting a small business, making investments, and creating a nest egg for retirement. Family members and others could add money to it. Total cost to the government would be about $24 billion a year—"a very small amount by the standards of federal programs," Boshara says, correctly.

- The most ambitious proposal by far comes from two professors at Yale Law School, Bruce Ackerman and Anne Alstott. They would provide a one-time grant of $80,000 to every American as he or she reached young adulthood.

  The money—in the form of a portfolio of stocks and bonds—would be provided in $20,000 increments each year for four consecutive years (at ages 21–24), with three exceptions: no high school diploma, no money; a criminal record would, or at least could, reduce your disbursements; and if you attend college you could withdraw up to $20,000 per year beginning freshman year.

  I spoke with Alstott shortly after the book came out and asked, Why $80,000? She said she was afraid anything less than that would fail to inspire young people.

  The Ackerman-Alstott proposal would cost real money— $255 billion a year, about two-thirds of our military budget. To pay for it, they suggest a "wealth tax," an annual 2 percent tax on everyone's assets (coupled with an $80,000 "wealth exemption," which would free about 60 percent of us from the tax). "We knew it would be a hard sell," Alstott told me. "But we felt it was the right thing—in terms of transferring money from people who've had really enormous opportunities over the last generation to middle- and working-class people."

  She also suggested a less contentious means of paying for the proposal—a national sales tax. And Nicolaus Tideman, economics professor at Virginia Tech, has suggested a third means: a tax on the use of our non-renewable natural resources. "I like to think they're everyone's common heritage," he says. "So using that tax to pay for stakeholder accounts makes perfect sense."

I think the Ackerman-Alstott proposal is too grandiose and that Kuttner's or even Boshara's proposal would accomplish the main goal: focusing young minds (and especially poor kids' minds) on the fact that, if they make the right decisions with their stakeholder accounts, their futures can be bright.

When it comes to helping the poor, the national debate is as full of "soft-hearted" leftists and "tough-minded" conservatives as it was when I was a civil rights worker 40 years ago. By giving everyone a financial stake in their future and by guaranteeing every American a job, the radical middle would finally take us beyond the left-right debate and into a world where nobody will lose out on the American dream for lack of opportunity.

RESOURCES

Texts

For a moving general statement of the radical middle position on equality—rejecting "egalitarianism at all costs" and calling instead for a society that would cultivate people's capabilities—see Anthony Giddens, "The Question of Inequality," chap. 4 in *The Third Way and Its Critics* (2000). For a pragmatic, radical middle version of the argument that government should create public-sector jobs for unemployed citizens, see Nancy Rose, "Workfare vs. Fair Work: Public Job Creation," *Uncommon Sense* (May 1997), accessible online. For the more usual radical middle position that government should create jobs by providing various incentives to private employers, see Robert Haveman, "Equity with Employment," *Boston Review* (Summer 1997), accessible online; Matthew Miller, "Uncle Sam (Not Your Boss) Guarantees You a Living Wage," chap. 8 in *The Two Percent Solution* (2003); and Edmund Phelps, *Rewarding Work* (1997).

Among the various proposals for "nest eggs" for young people, see especially Anne Alstott and Bruce Ackerman, *The Stakeholder Society* (1999); Ray Boshara, "The $6,000 Solution," *Atlantic Monthly* (January-February 2003); Robert Kuttner, "Rampant Bull: Toward Wealth Endowments," *American Prospect* (July-August 1998); and Michael Sherraden, *Assets and the Poor* (1991).

Groups

Society for the Advancement of Socio-Economics (www.sase.org) is full of scholars and activists immersed in the issues raised here. National Jobs for All Coalition (www.njfac.org) is an advocate of government-created or -funded jobs. Four advocates of stakeholder accounts are the Asset Building Program of New America Foundation (www.newamerica.net), Center for Social Development (accessible online), Corporation for Enterprise Development (www.cfed.org), and RESULTS (www.results.org).

PART FOUR

MAXIMIZE
HUMAN POTENTIAL

10

CORPORATIONS
WE CAN BE PROUD OF

THREE DECADES AGO I attended a conference for political activists in the hills of New Hampshire and met two young men whom I came to love like brothers. Both Art and Marc were brilliant, and ambitious, and magnetic. And both were extraordinarily critical of corporations. But the ways they responded to the corporate threat—in the 30 years since that conference—couldn't have been more different.

Like many people on the left, Art saw corporations as corrupt and unmovable. Over time, Marc developed a more radical middle position. He began to see that, if you want to maximize human potential in this world, then corporations and businesses—where the vast majority of us work—have got to become part of the solution. And he began to understand that it's in corporations' own long-term interest to become smarter, less rigid, and more humanly appealing.

Art's and Marc's lives mirrored their convictions. Art publicly aligned himself with the Philadelphia counter-culture and, in the 1990s—without missing a beat—the antiglobalization movement. His tattered inner-city home became a much-appreciated crash pad for radicals from coast to coast. An ancient printing press, in what might otherwise have been his family's dining room, churned out passionate tracts against the profit motive, against nuclear power and the nuclear family, against the corporate suppression of research into alternative energy sources. No one really knew how Art paid his bills, but most of us assumed it was from some sort of trust fund.

Marc eventually left his rural commune, toured with a band for a while, then proceeded to learn from two radical middle thinkers from the corporate world—one of the best "win-win" negotiators we have (William Ury) and one of the best management consultants (John Kotter). And now he's traveling around the world doing extraordinary behind-the-scenes consulting and mediation with a galaxy of Fortune 500 companies (including some of the biggest), with major nonprofits, with investment companies, and even with people in Congress and the U.N.

You can draw many lessons from Art's and Marc's experiences. One is that, in the end, the world you take is equal to the world you make. But there's more than a New Age lesson to be drawn here. Art became a footnote, at best, and Marc became a Player, not least of all because Marc was right and Art was wrong about the kind of corporate problem we're facing.

Most conservatives and liberals see corporate misbehavior as the result of "bad apples." So the reforms they support—such as those written into the Sarbanes-Oxley Act (Congress's bipartisan response to the Enron scandals)—are limited and grudging.

For radicals and antiglobalists like Art, the problem is not bad apples but "rotten roots": the corporate world is inherently corrupt and evil. "The Enron scandal provided a rare public window into the depth of the corruption of the ruling institutions of the suicide economy," says antiglobalist leader David Korten. As a result, the antiglobalists' suggested reforms tend to be more punitive than constructive. For example, the Program on Corporations, Law & Democracy (POCLAD), one of the most prominent anti-corporate NGOs, would ban corporations from "all discussion and debate about public policy" and deny corporations "the privilege of owning other corporations." (That'll fix 'em!)

Radical middle thinkers take a third position that borrows from— but is no mushy compromise between—the Establishment and radical positions.

Like conservatives and liberals, we admire the business institutions that have gradually evolved in this country, such as limited-liability corporations and the stock market. We find it disturbing that most corporate critics have no real affection for corporations, no real

sense of their history, and no real appreciation of what they've contributed to economic progress. We'd rather improve those institutions than waste precious time and energy trying to uproot and
replace them with whatever antiglobalist enthusiasms Naomi Klein
and David Korten are proffering at the moment (community-only
businesses? "cooperative" forms of organization? alternative money
systems?).

However, like the antiglobalists, radical middle-ists are committed to getting at the roots of our corporate problems. And we're
committed to moving toward a galvanizing vision—albeit a real-
world vision that would make actually existing corporations enjoy-
able places to work and appropriate places from which to serve
society.

Here's how I and the rest of the radical middle understand our
corporate challenge:

- Corporate culture is at the root of our corporate problems.
Capitalism or the "corporate form" is not;
- You can reform corporate culture directly, by bringing in consultants;
- At the same time, you can reform corporate culture indirectly,
by passing laws that don't "punish" corporations but do contribute to steering corporate culture in the right direction.

I am *not* saying corporations should be more "socially responsible." Guilting corporations into coughing up $10,000 for the local
park or $100,000 for the NAACP is not what the radical middle is
about. I am saying it's in corporations' own bottom-line interest to
focus on creating long-term wealth, not short-term shareholder
value; and that the way to induce them to do that is to induce them
to change their cultures; and that smart old consultants and smart
new laws are both integral to that process.

IT'S THE CULTURE, STUPID

Max Weber was right and Karl Marx was wrong, says historian David
Landes. "If we learn anything from the history of economic development, it is that culture makes almost all the difference."

Culture plays an especially dominant role in business "since all businesses are people businesses," say corporate culture gurus Terrence Deal and Allan Kennedy. "Companies that focus on their people and create a culture in which employees can thrive achieve superior, long-term business success."

Unfortunately, the culture in most American companies—never that great to begin with—has by most accounts, including Deal and Kennedy's, been going downhill. And the reason isn't hard to find: short-term greed is increasingly winning out over concern for long-term value.

At Enron, top executives routinely took home tens of millions of dollars a year, even after it became clear that the company was on the brink of financial collapse. And the greed wasn't confined to the top. One executive told *Fortune* magazine that Enron traders were afraid to go to the bathroom because the trader sitting next to them might peek at their screen to trade against them.

There was a maniacal focus on short-term profit. TV monitors throughout the Enron building displayed the stock price at all times. In a bitter e-mail to CEO Ken Lay, one Enron energy trader complained, "Enron Energy Services only manages quarter to quarter. They are reactive, not proactive."

You rarely find short-term obsession without arrogance, and Enron proved no exception. A banner in Enron's lobby proclaimed, "The World's Leading Company." An in-house spoof video made in 1997 (and later leaked to the *Wall Street Journal*) recounted how in the year 2020 Enron was elected "the world's first global governing body."

Even Enron's own special investigative subcommittee reported—after Enron had gone belly-up—that Enron had generated "a culture that appears to have encouraged pushing the limits."

Antiglobalists are arguing that Enron's short-sighted arrogance and greed is the future of American corporate capitalism. Their argument rests on the widespread notion that it's against the law for American corporations to operate on any basis other than by maximizing short-term profit for shareholders (aka "shareholder value"). As David Korten almost gleefully puts it, all corporations are under a legal imperative to "behave like cancers [and] maximize financial returns to absentee owners without regard to the consequences for people or planet."

That notion is false, though. The theory of shareholder value maximization is just that—a theory, nothing more. It's never been written into black-letter law. I once told readers of my newsletter that I'd eat my words if any of them could send me one final court decision from the last 50 years holding that directors cannot run a corporation from the perspective of what they sincerely consider to be the long-term, broad-gauge interests of the shareholders; and though I received more than the usual amount of invective from radicals, I received zero citations of legal opinions.

BRING IN THE CONSULTANTS

The radical middle goal is to turn corporations into organizations that maximize the human potential of their employees—and maximize their own potential to serve the long-term interests of us all. The radical middle method is to change corporate culture accordingly. One way to change corporate culture is by bringing in consultants who are smart, experienced, and personally formidable enough to convince corporate managers to adopt humane, long-term views of their companies.

That is already beginning to happen—significantly, at the corporations' own behest (post-Enron, they themselves know that "something" is wrong). Among the leading radical-middle–oriented consultants these days are:

> • *Peter Senge.* Senge not only introduced the concept of the "learning organization" to corporate managers (and particularly Baby Boom managers, who took to the concept like ducks to water), he gave the concept of the learning organization enough intellectual heft to outlast the "fad" stage and become a full-fledged theoretical alternative to the concept of the quick-make-a-buck-and-get-out-while-you-can organization.
>
> In Senge's view, learning organizations continually engage all their members—including their bottom-most members—in creating good and useful and original works. All members of learning organizations learn to engage in systems thinking, learn to engage in lifelong learning that includes (but goes beyond)

personal mastery, learn to engage in what the left used to call
"praxis" (thinking critically about what you do), and come to create—and continually re-create—positive, shared visions of their
preferred organizational future. If you've ever wondered why
some corporate types are actually excited by what they do,
chances are good they're part of a learning organization.

It's a myth that corporations can't learn. Marjorie Kelly, editor
of *Business Ethics Magazine* (and an advisor to my *Radical Middle
Newsletter*), publishes a list each year of the "Best Corporate Citizens" among our 1,000 largest publicly traded firms. Some of her
criteria are admirably conventional: total return to shareholders
(capital gains plus dividends), benefits to customers, impact on
employees. Others are more imaginative: impact on the home
community, on the environment, on non-U.S. stakeholders.

What's striking about the results is that many of the same
companies appear near the top each year. Among them: General
Mills, Hewlett-Packard, IBM, Intel, and Procter & Gamble. Call
them the "aspiring radical middle corporations."

• *Clement Bezold and Peter Schwartz.* Futurist consultants like
Bezold (Institute for Alternative Futures) and Schwartz (Global
Business Network) encourage corporations to engage in "scenario planning." That's not your father's top-down, bureaucratic
planning.

Scenario planning typically engages many members of an organization in creating "alternative images" for the future of their
organization. Bezold often encourages his clients to develop four
types of scenarios: "business as usual," "hard times," "visionary"
(hyperidealistic), and "transformational" (more or less radical
middle). Creating these scenarios requires corporate members
to question their deepest assumptions about how the world
works, and what they want the future to bring.

• *James Collins.* According to Collins, author of two of the bestselling business management books of our time (*Built to Last*
and *Good to Great*), the impulse to seek "More than Profits" is
one of the eight key traits of successful and long-lasting American companies.

"Contrary to business school doctrine," says this refugee from Stanford Business School, "we did not find 'maximizing shareholder wealth' or 'profit maximization' as the dominant driving force" of successful companies. "They have tended to produce a cluster of objectives, of which making money is only one—and not necessarily the primary one."

• *Daniel Goleman*. Most of us think of Goleman as the author of the global bestseller *Emotional Intelligence;* few realize he went on to become one of the most innovative management consultants in the U.S.

In a series of follow-up books, and through his consulting firm, he's been urging corporate managers to develop leaders with the capacity for "recognizing [their] own feelings and those of others." He'd go so far as to have corporations provide what he terms Emotional Competence Training to all their employees, top to bottom; and employ "training officers" to work with employees one-on-one over the years. The underlying idea is simple: emotionally healthy employees will make better-quality and more future-focused decisions.

It is extraordinary that few books on politics ever discuss the work of radical middle business consultants. Arguably, they're beginning to have a greater effect on corporate behavior than most laws could. And their influence is bound to grow in the years ahead, as increasing numbers of caring people enter business and the professions (see Part Six below).

BRING ON THE GOOD LAWS

Unfortunately, it's not enough to change corporate culture through consultants. It may not be illegal for corporations to take a long-term view of their future, but some laws do make that goal more difficult. And so does the absence of certain laws.

We need radical middle consultants on the inside. But on the outside, we need less hopeful talk about corporate social responsibility, and more straight talk about structural (legally enforceable) approaches to corporate accountability.

Radical middle thinkers are on the case. While Congress has been patting itself on the back for passing the Sarbanes-Oxley bill, sensible and visionary scholar-consultants like Jeffrey Garten (Yale School of Management), Allan Kennedy (*The End of Shareholder Value*), and Lawrence Mitchell (George Washington University Law School) have been assiduously suggesting laws and regulations that could induce every corporate pacesetter—executives, directors, accountants, and investors—to move from a short-term culture to a long-term culture:

Executives.
Sarbanes-Oxley failed to require companies to expense stock options—a huge mistake. (Stock options give the holder the right to buy a company's stock at a specific price and sell at the market price on the same day, and pocket the difference.) At least three-quarters of executive compensation is in stock options now, not pay. Options cost companies nothing—they are "free" to issue—and companies are not required to count them as an expense.

The losers are the company's stockholders, whose holdings are diluted when options are converted to stock. In addition, the losers are all investors and potential investors since a company's financial records are distorted when options go unrecorded. For example, Professor Garten claims that treating options as an expense would have reduced the reported earnings of the Standard & Poor's 500 companies by nearly 25 percent between 1995 and 2000.

Worse than any of that, though, from a radical middle perspective, is that stock options can motivate an executive to work toward boosting a company's stock price *now,* rather than work toward creating a healthy and sustainable company for the long term. Enron's managers—Ken Lay, Jeff Skilling, and the rest—are Exhibit A, but it's a huge temptation for executives everywhere.

For radical middle thinkers, the key question is how to make executive compensation more consistent with the creation of long-term value. So while it's important to have companies record stock option grants as a company expense, we can't stop there.

One idea is to preclude top executives from selling their company stock (whether acquired from options or not) so long as they remain in management or serve as consultants to the corporation. And possibly for one or two years thereafter.

Another good idea is to amend the tax laws so stock issued under option plans would be taxed more preferentially if an executive sold it after a lengthy holding period. That idea may be more purely radical middle, since it efficiently induces rather than simply forces responsible behavior.

Boards of directors.

Sarbanes-Oxley bans boards from making personal loans to top executives. Great. What it doesn't do, though, is induce boards to take any positive steps toward overseeing the long-term viability of the companies they supposedly oversee. How can that be done?

One way is by having boards stand for election every two or three years, or even every five years, rather than every year (but allow stockholders to recall board members for malfeasance at any time). That would build greater trust and understanding between boards and stockholders—and give boards greater leeway to plan for the long term rather than sweat over quarterly profits.

We might also figure out ways to encourage institutional investors (including mutual funds, insurance companies, and union pension funds) to stick with companies when they see that directors and officers have a long-term perspective . . . even when short-term profits are not what they could be.

Accountants.

Many observers have noted that Sarbanes-Oxley wimped out with regard to accountants. (Companies don't have to change accounting firms every five years—only accounting partners from the same firm; auditors can still provide some business services to their audit clients.) What few observers have noted, though, is that Sarbanes-Oxley failed to rethink either what should be reported by accountants or how they should report it.

Congress could surely mandate that corporations regularly disclose information of special relevance to consumers, workers, and communities (to be audited along with the financials)—for example, all product liability claims brought by consumers, all incidents of carpal tunnel syndrome reported by workers, and how much styrofoam packaging was added to the host community's waste stream. If corporations had to make such information available in clear, comparable form and on a regular basis, through qualified independent sources (such as social and environmental assessment engineers), it might factor more heavily into their decisionmaking.

Another idea whose time has come is for the SEC to revise accounting rules so long-term investments aren't treated as short-term costs. Some employment costs should surely be seen as investments in long-term increased productivity; and some R&D investments should surely be seen as down payments on future profits. (As it is now, both employment costs and R&D immediately detract from the bottom line. Yet stock options don't. Amazing.)

Investors.

Possibly the biggest single thing that can be done to combat the short-term culture of American business is to lower or eliminate taxes on gains from shares held several years. (Of course, to balance the effect of such a tax cut, income taxes for the wealthy should be increased.)

If we used a sliding scale, we could gradually reduce the tax on stock profits the longer the stock was held. We could even eliminate taxation on stock held over the very long term.

Not only would this give everyone incentives to invest for the long term. It would diminish short-term pressure on corporate managers, enabling them to plan for the long-term. And it would do more. It would encourage investors to pay much closer attention to the long-term plans and prospects of the corporations they invest in. Overnight, they'd become the strongest advocates of future-focused, humane, and sustainable corporate cultures.

Conservatives aren't demanding enough of our corporations. Liberals and antiglobalists want to shackle them. Only the radical middle wants to induce them to take the practical but visionary steps that could get them to an accountable, humane, and future-focused corporate culture.

Our corporations won't flourish without that culture. And if they don't flourish, neither will we.

My friend Art fought the good fight against the Big, Bad Corporations. Marx, or maybe Gandhi, will usher him out of this cruel vale with a smile. But my friend Marc got the last laugh: along with thousands of other radical middle thinkers and consultants and corporate executives, he's helping turn corporate America into something we may eventually be proud of.

RESOURCES

Texts

For a general understanding and appreciation of corporations from a radical middle perspective, see Terrence Deal and Allan Kennedy, *The New Corporate Cultures* (1999); Jeffrey Garten, *The Mind of the CEO* (2001); Art Kleiner, *The Age of Heretics: Heroes, Outlaws, and the Forerunners of Corporate Change* (1996); C. K. Prahalad and Kenneth Lieberthal, "The End of Corporate Imperialism," *Harvard Business Review* (July-August 1998); Robert Solomon, *A Better Way to Think About Business* (1999); and James Watson et al., *Golden Arches East* (1998).

For a good cross-section of the views of radical middle corporate consultants, see James Collins and Jerry Porras, *Built to Last* (1994); Daniel Goleman, *Working with Emotional Intelligence* (1998); John Kotter, *Leading Change* (1996); James Ogilvy, *Creating Better Futures* (2002); and Peter Senge, *The Fifth Discipline: The Art and Practice of the Learning Organization* (1990). For radical middle suggestions on corporate restructuring, see Margaret Blair, *Ownership and Control* (1995); Ralph Estes, *Tyranny of the Bottom Line* (1996); Jeffrey Garten, *The Politics of Fortune* (2002); Allan Kennedy, *The End of Shareholder Value* (2000); and Lawrence Mitchell, *Corporate Irresponsibility* (2001).

Groups

Organizations that see the world through this chapter's eyes include Association for Quality and Participation (www.aqp.org), Center for Corporate Citizenship (www.bc.edu/centers/ccc), Developing a Learning Society Project of the Institute for Alternative Futures (www.altfutures.com), Global Business Network (www.gbn.org), Society for Organizational Learning (www.solonline.org), and Tom Peters Company (www.tom peters.com).

11

LONG LIVE BIOTECH—
WITH ADULT SUPERVISION

O NE OF THE LAST THINGS I did in 1992 before leaving my alternative newsletter for law school was ask a man at my local grocery to tell me if he sold any fruits or vegetables that had been genetically engineered. Because if he did, I rather pompously explained, then he really needed to label them, because biotechnology was a Bad Thing. I'm not sure he even knew what biotechnology was. But he reassured me that he didn't carry anything remotely like that.

Flash forward 10 years. I ask Jim, my local grocer, to tell me if he sells any biotech foods—because I want to try them out!

The world hadn't changed, I'd changed. Law school teaches you to appreciate the power of rational, left-brain thinking and the glory of inductive reasoning, so I'd finally overcome my fear and suspicion of science and technology. It's a feeling many Americans share—in part because of our too often poorly taught high school science classes.

It's a feeling we should all try to overcome. A genetic new world is calling us, and it is full of extraordinary promise. But we'll need to proceed with knowledge and wisdom and care.

Bite into a genetically engineered apple and it really could, in the not too distant future, cure what ails you. Go inside my cells and alter my genes and keep me from ending up with cystic fibrosis. Grow golden rice in Southeast Asia and watch the scourge of Vitamin A deficiency (a principal cause of blindness) disappear.

If done right, biotechnology can enhance the entire world's well-being. And that's why the radical middle is drawn to it. One of our key value commitments is maximizing human potential.

Unfortunately, other agendas are at work when it comes to biotech. Because it's such an intimate subject—it is, literally, about the essence of life itself—it's become a magnet for extremists, and the national biotech debate has begun to verge on the ridiculous.

Many of those who support genetic modification of plants and humans are incorrigibly optimistic. Where thoughtful people see shades of gray, bio-optimists see only sunshine. "Breakthroughs in genetic engineering are no different from any other form of technological or social progress," purrs a man from Novartis, the big pharmaceutical company. Self-interested supporters of biotech have their own lobbying and PR group, the Biotechnology Industry Organization, "BIO" for short, and they have plenty of moles among academics and futurists.

Many of those who oppose biotech are beyond pessimistic—they're downright hostile. Some of them associate biotech with white, male, American imperialism, as when Columbia law professor Patricia Williams fulminates in *The Nation* against "scientist-explorers plant[ing] an infinity of little flags in [the genetic] New World." A hipper brand of hostility finds its way into places like *Slate*, the online magazine, where William Saletan issues ominous warnings about new ammunition for "racists" (because genetic differences may exist among the races). And, of course, Jeremy Rifkin is against the inhuman practice of genetic engineering, just as he was against the inhuman practice of *in vitro* fertilization back in 1978. And Amory Lovins sees a moral equivalence between biotech and nuclear weapons. And there are groups like "Biodevastation," and books by science writers with titles like *Genetic Engineering, Dream or Nightmare?: Turning the Tide on the Brave New World of Bad Science and Big Business*.

Although the biotech debate may seem hopelessly polarized, a third voice—nuanced, hopeful, adult—has begun to be heard. Call it the voice of cautious optimism. Call it the voice of the radical middle.

You can hear the new voice in certain pronouncements of the Center for Science in the Public Interest, a major nutrition-oriented public interest group, whose Biotech Project recently broke with the antiglobalist left and declared that genetically engineered crops "could be a boon to farmers and consumers, especially in developing countries." You can hear it in the United Nations Development Program's recent warning that "if the development community turns its back on the explosion of technological innovation in food [and] medicine, it risks marginalizing itself." And you can hear it in recent books by unusually thoughtful scientists—among them, Paul Lurquin, Lee Silver, Gregory Stock, and Mark Winston.

Devour these complex, cautiously optimistic sources and you'll find yourself embracing a radical middle approach to biotechnology. An approach that emphasizes the alleviation of human suffering and the advancement of the human spirit—even as it insists upon careful government monitoring of both plant and human biotech initiatives.

COMING TO GRIPS WITH BIOTECH: NEW FOODS

Genetic engineering of foods—"biotech" foods—means you can take genes from one organism (such as a flower or vegetable or fish) and add it to the genetic material of any other organism. That's different from traditional plant breeding in which the genes of only closely related organisms can be exchanged.

Our stunning new capacity to manipulate traits across organisms is full of opportunities for us:

- We can take insect-killing toxins from bacteria (such as Bt) and insert them into plants (such as corn), and insects that try to eat the plants will be killed. Presto: farmers would have to spray little or no pesticide, and farm workers would have to encounter little or no pesticide.
- We can take genes that prevent weed-killing herbicides from affecting crops, and insert them into crops. Voila: farmers could kill weeds infinitely more cheaply and easily than they do now.
- We can insert genes that'll make crops frost- and drought-resistant. Farmers would have longer growing seasons, and nations could expand their agricultural regions.

If you insert nutrient-producing genes into crops, you'll be able to prevent malnutrition syndromes (caused by deficiencies in vitamin

A, vitamin E, and iron). Insert other genes and you'll be able to increase the storage lifetime for fruits and vegetables. Insert yet other genes and you'll be able to produce pharmaceutical-producing crops, so people would be able to protect themselves against dread diseases simply by eating an apple or a banana.

The downside, of course, is that some or all of this might be dangerous. And neither side in the ongoing biotech debate is particularly helpful here. One side tends to be shocked—shocked—that we'd even consider cutting back on "progress" (biotech) because of our petty doubts and reservations. The other side is so unwilling to proceed in the face of uncertainty, and so convinced that our scientists have been bought off by industry, that it won't rest until genetic engineering of foods has been banned or sharply curtailed.

But the evidence so far is that biotech food is safe. "There have been no proven health-related problems from GM foods to date," says biologist Mark Winston in his exemplary radical middle book, *Travels in the Genetically Modified Zone*. "[Even] the StarLink incident [whereby biotech corn for animals got mixed in with other corn] was caused by regulatory laxity rather than problems with analytical methods." Recently, the National Academy of Sciences—in a report co-authored with the British, Brazilian, Chinese, Indian, and Mexican national academies—came to exactly the same conclusion.

Doug Gurian-Sherman of Center for Science in the Public Interest's Biotech Project (and a Ph.D. in plant pathology) emphasizes that biotech food is not only safe, consumers are actually benefiting from it because of the reduced use of pesticides. And if you're worried about yucky fish genes being inserted into plant genes, consider this: genetic research has revealed that different life forms already share a high percentage of the same genes. "Even plants and humans have many genes in common naturally," says a recent Congressional report.

The evidence suggests that biotech food is safe for the environment as well. Yes, there have been minor impacts on non-target insects and other organisms in the field, and there is some concern that herbicide-resistant genes that jump to non-biotech weeds or crops may in time produce so-called super-weeds (immune to many herbicides). But "none of these effects are any worse than those caused by conventional agricultural practices," says biologist Winston, "and the reduced pesticide use possible with [biotech] has to be considered a plus for the environment." Besides, with proper monitoring, farmers can be made to be more careful.

The developing world stands to benefit most from biotech foods. "Improving food security for the world's poorest farmers means improving their productivity," says Sakiko Fukuda-Parr, director of the U.N.'s Human Development Report office. "The new tools of biotechnology offer the potential for creating crop varieties that meet the challenges of farming that they face—such as varieties that are more tolerant of drought or saline soils."

Unlike opponents of biotech, radical middle policy analysts welcome these possibilities with open arms. We revel in science, technology, progress, fairly-won profit. We admire social change agents like the late civil rights leader Bayard Rustin—but we equally admire social change agents like vitamin-A-carrying Golden Rice creators Peter Beyer and Ingo Potrykus. Where we differ with conventional supporters of biotech is in the degree to which we'd provide strict oversight of biotech testing and implementation, and in the extent to which we'd ensure biotech is made readily available to even the poorest farmers in the developing world.

For example, many required tests are now performed by corporations and are merely "reviewed" by U.S. government agencies. Under a radical middle regime, all tests would be performed by government agencies.

The recent report by the National Academy of Sciences (NAS), cited above, catches the radical middle spirit. On the one hand, full speed ahead. On the other, have the government do "thorough risk assessment" of all biotech plant varieties as they're developed, then implement a "monitoring system to evaluate these risks" in subsequent field tests and releases. If developing nations lack the tools or resources to do this—make sure that they get them, pronto.

Center for Science in the Public Interest's Gurian-Sherman is on the same radical middle page as the NAS. He'd have the Environmental Protection Agency (EPA) thoroughly review every biotech plant that's "grown in a way that can affect the environment." Then, before any crops are turned into food, he'd have companies demonstrate to the Food and Drug Administration (FDA) that their crops "are not toxic, don't contain any allergens, and don't pose other risks." Both the FDA and the EPA would use tests recommended by an independent organization like the NAS. Finally, all procedures and test results would be open to the public.

In the developing world, the U.S. should do far more than it's currently doing to train biologists, fund research, and guarantee access to biotech patents.

"The available scientific methods can provide reasonable security about the safety" of biotech foods, says biologist Winston. The radical middle task is to make sure those methods are applied rigorously, fairly, and transparently.

COMING TO GRIPS WITH BIOTECH: NEW HUMANS?

The genetic lottery is cruel. For no good reason, some of us are born with low IQs or terrible mental afflictions; some of us are born with severe (or not so severe) physical deformities. Investigating the human genetic code is one of the great scientific passions of our time, and for good reason. It opens up extraordinary possibilities for human healing and self-design. Among them:

- *Genetic testing.* Researchers have already learned how to test for hundreds of genetic disorders in children and adults. Soon, a single test will be able to examine thousands of your genes and reveal whether any are defective or unusual.
- *Gene therapy.* Increasingly, it will be possible to correct serious diseases and disorders of children and adults (e.g., cystic fibrosis, albino skin pigment) by going inside cells and altering genes.
- *Prenatal testing.* Today, prenatal genetic testing is typically done when there's a risk for a disorder (e.g., because of family history). Soon, prenatal tests will be able to check for many genetic disorders and will become routine.
- *Genetic enhancement.* Someday, prenatal genetic testing may be used not only to avoid genetic disorders but as a preliminary step to altering genes to enhance desired features such as height, IQ, athletic ability, and temperament.

- *Germline therapy.* Someday, we'll be able to alter not only our genes, but the genes we pass on to our children (by altering the DNA that's copied and passed on through our eggs or sperm).

Many supporters of biotech tend to be gung-ho about all the above. "If it makes money, do it," is their counter-counter-cultural motto. Many opponents are actively hostile. They may or may not believe in God, but they sure don't want us to "play God." Those of us at the radical middle are—and should be—supportive of human biotech. But we're also treading carefully, with all senses alert.

For example, you'd think genetic testing and screening would be unalloyed goods. After a genetic test revealed a predisposition (for asthma, for example), we could change our behavior or alter our environment and be better off. But the real world is more complicated. Suppose a test revealed that you're carrying the gene for Huntington's disease and no treatment is available. What then? Or suppose a treatment is available but is well beyond your means? And who else should know you're carrying the gene? Your significant other? And at what point in the relationship?

Radical middle thinkers want everyone to have the choice of knowing whatever can be known about their physical conditions. But given the phenomenal sensitivities involved, we also want everyone to have access to members of a barely emerging and badly underfunded profession: genetic counseling. Counselors can help people think through ahead of time how different test results might affect them. Just as important, counselors can—I would say, must—be available once people get their results.

Prenatal testing is another area where you'd think caution could be thrown to the wind. If a fetus appears to be carrying a gene for a debilitating hereditary disease, everyone might be better off if the fetus is aborted. But there are all kinds of genetic disorders. Suppose your preborn child is at risk of developing conditions that are not debilitating but just socially undesirable? Or suppose genetic enhancement becomes available (and affordable)? Will parents keep having abortions until they feel they have a "perfect" fetus? Here again, I think genetic counselors will have a crucial psychological (not to mention spiritual and philosophical) role to play, along with everyone else in the parents' lives who has an ounce of sensitivity.

Opponents of biotech are of course apoplectic about the possibility of genetic enhancement. Even the Council for Responsible Genetics, one of the more measured oppositional groups, associates voluntary genetic enhancement with the Nazis. And don't even raise the possibility of germline therapy with biotech opponents. Jeremy Rifkin, for one, says germline would bring us to "the precipice of a eugenics era."

At the radical middle, we see germline differently. Some of our reasons are pragmatic. "If the disease allele is replaced in all cells," says philosopher of science Philip Kitcher, "descendants would be freed from the disease." That's not playing God. That's being compassionate. Sensible. Human.

Some of our reasons are science-based. Biotech opponents routinely claim germline will reduce the genetic variation among humans, but biologist Michael Reiss and moral philosopher Roger Straughan deftly counter that argument: "Germline therapy may one day lead to even more genetic variation as . . . parents opt for [different combinations of] genes in their children."

The human-identity argument is with the radical middle. Many biotech opponents' preferred vision of our identity—which you can glimpse in certain environmental groups—is one of timid humanity, fearful of its own powers and subordinate to nature. Many biotech supporters' vision is one of arrogant humanity, dominating nature. But the radical middle vision is that of humanity as co-creator with nature, and therefore rightfully concerned with its own self-exploration and self-improvement, just as nature is concerned with its own evolution. UCLA scientist Gregory Stock puts it well when he says, "To turn away from germline selection and modification without even exploring them would be to deny our essential nature and perhaps our destiny."

Even the social justice argument is with the radical middle. Some biotech opponents ask how we can think about genetic enhancements and germline therapy when there's "already" too much inequality in the world. But if a radical middle society ensures access to preventive health care and great teachers and good jobs (all things called for in this book), then that question not only loses its moral force, it gives way to its opposite: since genetics and environment both weigh heavily on our capacities, how can we *not* continually work at improving our genetic condition?

The one line in the sand that the radical middle draws here is that all our work in human biotech needs to be done with caution (just as it should be on the plant biotech side). Politically, that means the government must regulate and monitor all developments.

But that doesn't mean choking off genetic testing or gene therapy or even the experiments with germline therapy. We're not dealing with atomic weapons here—one mistake will not vaporize us. As many geneticists suggest, it would be wise to allow use of the technology and learn from what happens. In the land of the radical middle, transparency is king—or at least an important duke.

The polarized pro- and anti- voices in the biotech debate can make for great entertainment. But only the cautiously optimistic, radical middle voice speaks to the human condition. Our drive to understand and improve ourselves may be limitless—bioethicist Arthur Caplan reminds us it's prehistoric, and profoundly important—and we'd damage the human enterprise more by drawing back or waiting for some impossible social-political "consensus" than by moving cautiously forward. In the meantime, it's incumbent on us to come up with tough laws safeguarding genetic information and prohibiting genetic discrimination. If all goes well, we'll need them.

RESOURCES

Texts

For a broad radical middle overview of this subject, see Walter Truett Anderson, *Evolution Isn't What It Used to Be* (1996). For cautious optimism on biotech foods, see especially biologist Mark Winston's colorful and engaging *Travels in the Genetically Modified Zone* (2002). A bit more technical, but still comprehensible, is biologist Paul Lurquin's *High Tech Harvest: Understanding Genetically Modified Food Plants* (2002). See also United Nations Development Program, *Human Development Report 2001: Making New Technologies Work for Human Development* (2001), and National Academy of Sciences, *Transgenic Plants and World Agriculture* (2000), both accessible online.

For thoughtful optimism on human biotech, see Kyla Dunn, "The Life (and Death?) of Cloning," *Atlantic Online* (22 May 2002); William Haseltine, "Regenerative Medicine: A Future Healing Art," *Brookings Review* (Winter 2003), accessible online; Matt Ridley, *Genome* (1999); Lee Silver, *Remaking Eden* (1997); and Gregory Stock, *Redesigning Humans: Choosing Our Genes, Changing Our Future* (2002).

Groups

Radical middle approaches to food biotech are espoused by the Biotechnology Project at Center for Science in the Public Interest (www.cspinet.org) and the International Food Policy Research Institute (www.ifpri.org). Radical middle approaches to human biotech can be found at Center for Bioethics (www.bioethics.net) and Center for Society, the Individual and Genetics (www.arc2.ucla.edu/csig).

12

BRING BACK THE DRAFT, FOR EVERYONE THIS TIME

YEAH, THAT WAS ME in the American Flag apron, cooking spaghetti or meat loaf or (God help us) horse stew for 35 super-hungry people. At the time I was running the Harriet Tubman Memorial Hostel, better known as The Last Resort, the big hostel in Vancouver, Canada, for U.S. draft dodgers and military deserters. Just before that I'd co-founded and directed the Toronto Anti-Draft Programme, Canada's major draft dodger assistance organization, and written a controversial underground bestseller, the *Manual for Draft-Age Immigrants to Canada*. And a while before that I'd shredded my draft card.

So why was it that, in the late 1990s, I was petitioning the Army's Legal Services Agency to waive its age requirement (the ceiling is age 35) and let me enlist in the JAG Corps, the Army's lawyer corps? Why was it that I'd offered to serve in Korea or Bosnia, not most soldiers' favorite destinations?

I'm still not entirely sure. I've always felt good about refusing to fight in Vietnam. I'd dreamed of becoming a great American historian (with a holistic and internationalist bent). But it was inconceivable to me—I mean, not even an option—that I would answer my country's call to go off and try to kill, maim, and intimidate Vietnamese for no good reason. Even in 1965–66, it was plain to anyone who made any sincere effort to look into the situation that the Vietnam war would do unbearable damage to both countries.

If you refused to go to Vietnam, and you didn't object to war on religious grounds, there were only two stand-up, non-Clintonesque alternatives open to you: jail or Canada. I chose Canada because I thought I could save more Vietnamese and American lives working against the war machine from Toronto than I could sitting in some federal penitentiary.

Still, there I was, 30 years later, sending my JAG application in to the Army. Part of what I wrote can provide a clue to what I wanted:

"Age may or may not bring wisdom. But it has given me the opportunity to see my actions in perspective, and even though I know I did right by going to Canada, I still feel in my heart a need to fulfill my duty to my country."

MAKING "DUTY" RELEVANT TO THE 21ST CENTURY

"Duty to country"—the phrase has an archaic ring to it. The language of duties and responsibilities has given way to a language of rights and grievances today. But I think most of us secretly know—and those of us at the radical middle are inclined to say—that without such concepts as duty and honor and service, no civilization can endure.

Yes, Republicans and Democrats still trot out the rhetoric of duty and service when it suits their partisan purposes. But in the end, neither party steers its ship by that stuff. Quietly, our politicians have been paying more and more in wages and benefits just to keep the number of "voluntary" military recruits relatively stable. (The pay ratio between a master sergeant and a private has fallen from 7:1 to less than 3:1 since the draft era ended.) And no politician will say it on the record during the current terrorist menace, but it's well known in Washington that the quality of recruits is on the decline. Meanwhile, the Democrats' vaunted national service initiative, AmeriCorps, employs only 50,000 volunteers, many at haplessly menial jobs, and the vast majority of Americans have never heard of it.

It is time for our political leaders to stop making ritual noises about duty and honor and service, and attempt to reinvent those concepts for the 21st century.

The way to reinvent those concepts for a nation increasingly made up of knowledge workers and caring persons is to institute a draft that allows for some individual choice—and that reaches every single one of us.

I suspect Americans would respond positively to a frank and un-shirkable call to duty and service, if it gives us some choice in how we exercise that duty and service. Say, if it gives young people a choice between military service, homeland defense, and community service. (Exactly the kind of choice my generation did *not* have during the Vietnam war.)

Wouldn't it be wonderful for a radical middle political leader to stand up and say to young Americans, "There are no free rides in life, and it's incumbent on you—you who are enjoying the fruits of past generations' sacrifices—to either contribute some time to this country's defense, or contribute some time to healing its wounds."

Similar things have been said by wise Americans from diverse political viewpoints—but we weren't ready to listen. In the early 20th century, psychologist William James and journalist Randolph Bourne urged versions of "universal national service" on us, versions of conscription that would have allowed us to choose between military and civilian service. In the summer of 1940, Eleanor Roosevelt argued for a "wider service" that would have sent some draftees out to be teachers and community revitalizers. But all those proposals disappeared down the great American memory hole.

In the Sixties, people ranging from anthropologist Margaret Mead to Defense Secretary Robert McNamara proposed tying civilian service to the draft. Their proposals disappeared down that same hole.

During the Seventies, liberal Republican Rep. Pete McCloskey (Calif.) issued passionate calls for national service.

In the 1980s, Northwestern University military sociologist Charles Moskos proposed a spinoff of the universal national service idea: every American who wanted federal financial aid for college would have to perform military or civilian service. By and by, Senator Sam Nunn and Rep. David McCurdy proposed a watered-down version of Moskos, President Clinton proposed a watered-down version of Nunn-McCurdy, the House and Senate further diluted the idea, and in the end we got a re-tooled version of VISTA (Volunteers in Service to America, the domestic Peace Corps), AmeriCorps.

Beginning (perhaps not coincidentally) with the election of an alleged draft evader as President in 1992, and continuing through the presidency of an alleged combat shirker, people are again beginning to broach the real universal national service idea. Given my experience, which was the prototypical Baby Boomer experience—wanting to serve, but not necessarily wanting to serve by slaughtering politically objectionable Vietnamese and their families and neighbors—the time for mandatory national service offering military and civilian options may have come. Couple that with increasing numbers of people valuing rich personal experiences *and* social service, and you've got the makings of a successful radical middle policy initiative.

Symbolically, none could be better. It's an initiative that combines the idealism of the left with the patriotism of the right; the sense of obligation normally associated with conservatism, with the freedom-to-set-one's-own-course normally associated with liberalism. And what you end up with is no mushy middle. It is genuinely off the old political spectrum: mandatory national service for all young people—no exceptions—but with everyone free to choose among military, homeland security, and community options.

How supportive is the general public? Recently, Rasmussen Research asked a cross-section of Americans whether every 18-year-old should be required to perform *two years* of mandatory government service (longer than most policy analysts are suggesting). Those under 30 rejected the idea by a two-to-one margin, but the split was only 16 percent to 8 percent. The vast majority of twentysomethings didn't have a strong opinion one way or the other. And those over 65 favored the idea by a 49 percent to 36 percent margin. Probably a lot more people would favor the idea once an attractive plan was presented to them, and once the benefits—political and personal—were set forth.

PLANNING FOR DUTY

At least seven plans for mandatory national service (but allowing all draftees to choose between civilian and military service) have been presented over the last decade or so, and it's probably fair to describe every one of the presenters as radical middle—sociologist Amitai Etzioni, political scientist Robin Gerber, journalist Paul Glastris, military commentator Col. David Hackworth (ret.), author Mickey Kaus, policy analyst Michael Lind, and sociologist Charles Moskos.

In addition, President Clinton's Secretary of the Army, Louis Caldera, floated the idea of a joint citizen-service / military draft at a National Press Club briefing in March 1999. And New York liberal Rep. Charles Rangel (D-N.Y.) is advocating a traditional military draft that would require all those not selected for military service to perform civilian national service. To give you a sense of how completely the mandatory national service idea cuts across ideological lines, consider that the chief sponsor of Rangel's bill in the Senate is South Carolina conservative Democrat Fritz Hollings.

The seven proposals differ—but not as much as you might think. My own proposal borrows from the best of all of them while adding certain humane twists of my own devising:

Y'all come.
Draft everyone on their 18th birthday or—if they're still in high school at 18—then right after high school or on their 20th birthday, whichever comes first. That's *everyone,* pardner—male or female, rich or poor, gay or straight, smart or dumb, physically fit or physically challenged.

Training.
Give everyone some basic military training, or—if they object to military training—then training in nonviolent resistance and defense. Col. Hackworth puts it nicely when he says, "In boot camp, they'll learn the basics—drill, discipline, teamwork, leadership, responsibility, and citizenship—while getting physically hard and mentally together."

Options.
Then, give everyone a choice: one year in community service, two years in homeland security, or three years in the military (but, of course, no one judged unfit for homeland or military service could go into them). Finish training everyone according to the type of service they've signed up for.

Compensation.
Those in community service would get subsistence stipends; those in homeland security service would get much higher pay; those in

military service would get a World War Two type GI bill upon dis-
charge. In effect, those who put their life on the line for three years
would get to join the knowledge society, or—alternately—get a leg
up in starting a small business or purchasing a home. Rome fell in
part because it couldn't induce its own citizens to engage in its defense. A radical middle society would not be so proud or so ostrich-
like as to make that mistake.

Military tasks.

Most Pentagon officials do not want to return to a military draft.
But there's no need to choose between a professional military and a
draft. Even if actual combat is left to professional soldiers and their
high-tech weapons, hundreds of thousands of important combat-
support tasks could be performed by draftees. In addition, it only
takes basic training plus four months of special police training to
send peacekeepers out into the field. Working in close consultation
with our allies (and, hopefully, the U.N.), we'll be able to contribute draftees to Bosnia, Kosovo, Liberia, and other places where
genocidal wars have broken out or are threatening to break out,
such as Israel-Palestine.

Homeland security tasks.

Few politicians are eager to admit how many people we'll need on
the homeland defense side to really do things right. A draft can't
provide more police officers, firefighters, and emergency medical
technicians, but it can provide the hundreds of thousands more
uniformed men and women we'll need to ensure homeland security. We are going to need them to guard airports, dams, power
plants, sports facilities, and embassies. We are going to need them
patrolling the border, we are going to need them as agents tracking
down illegal immigrants, we are going to need them inspecting
ships, we are going to need them as air marshals.

Community service tasks.

Draftees who choose to be on the community side *must not* be assigned to make-work projects. Many of our greatest national defense
tasks (broadly defined) are civilian rather than military. To focus on

the most pressing tasks—and to keep conflicts with unions to a minimum—we could organize all community service draftees into nine distinct "corps," as follows:

- Inner-city corps. To repair public spaces, maintain the physical condition of public spaces, and check for and clean up lead paint.
- Police corps. To patrol public spaces, collect child-support payments, and provide escorts for seniors.
- Hospital corps. To serve as nurses' aides.
- Education corps. To serve as teaching assistants, work in day care centers, and tutor young people.
- Environmental corps. To facilitate urban recycling, clean up urban parks, and clean up the rural environment. (With proper supervision, many of these important tasks could be done by those with mental or physical infirmities.)
- Assisting-the-elderly corps. To help the infirm in nursing homes, to comfort them, and to provide home care for those who can avoid nursing homes if they get such care.
- Infrastructure corps. To help contractors rebuild our crumbling infrastructure.
- Peace corps. To expand the existing Peace Corps' presence tenfold.
- Vietnam-era corps (for older volunteers only). To find appropriately challenging and useful tasks for all those Vietnam-era draft evaders, military deserters, and combat shirkers who still long to fulfill their duty to country.

Duty's Promise

Besides the practical security and community benefits detailed above, mandatory national service would help us maximize our potential as individuals and as a nation.

True, with mandatory service we'd have to give up at least one year to a cause greater than ourselves. But what we'd lose in perfect freedom we'd more than make up for in other ways.

Today, most of us march in lockstep from grade to grade and then through college or right into the world of work. Mandatory service would force us to take a deep breath, find our bearings, get a better grasp on what we wanted from life.

Mickey Kaus captures another key benefit in three words: "Salvage impoverished youths."

America may be the most diverse country on Earth—the whole world is here. But growing up, few of us know it because of our segregated housing patterns and lifestyles. Mandatory service—if it's truly universal—would mix all races, classes, and temperaments in a common endeavor. "It might act as a leveling influence," Army Secretary Caldera told the National Press Club, "and help bring our country closer on the basis of a shared experience—bearing the burdens of providing for our nation's security."

And can you think of a better character-building device? What better way to enhance ordinary people's sense of self-respect than by having them play an integral part in doing the most important thing a nation can do—protect itself and its allies around the world? And what better way to put into perspective the "me-first" mentality that's too often the flip side of American freedom?

DUTY: A COST/BENEFIT ANALYSIS

The economic costs of mandatory national service would not be exorbitant. Sociologist Amitai Etzioni estimates that if every single 18-year-old participated, total cost would be $33 billion a year—$11,000 per person times three million people. Journalist Steven Waldman uses a Clinton aide's secret memo to estimate $12,000 per person per year—but even that works out to only $36 billion per year, less than one-tenth of the military budget.

And that's not counting deductions for salaries for young people who'd be in the military anyway; savings on welfare and unemployment; and savings from reduction in crime.

Indirect economic gains are likely to be even greater. Etzioni deftly gets at some of them when he says, "By encouraging and developing the virtues of hard work, responsibility, and cooperation . . . national service would . . . improve economic productivity. [And it] would probably provide young people with greater maturity and skills than they would normally have upon entering college or vocational training[, further] benefiting themselves and the community."

Moral gains should be added in too. A huge segment of my generation knows it didn't answer its country's call, and even though many of us are proud to have opposed the Vietnam war, many of us are not proud to have not served this country at all. In the Sixties, you either signed up to kill Vietnamese or you dodged (or more cleverly avoided) the draft. Those were your only choices. The result was a cynicism and alienation that many of us feel to this day.

Now many of our military personnel sign up not because they want to be soldiers, but because they need or want the benefits. And millions of crucial civilian tasks, from patrolling our borders to comforting infirm elderly, are going undone because we can't afford to pay for them through the formal economy. Everybody knows this, and that's feeding the cynicism of a new generation of Americans.

We need mandatory national service so we will all take part in performing the collective tasks we know are ours. We need mandatory national service because duty and honor are as necessary to us as oxygen and water.

That's what I was trying to tell the Army in my application to the JAG corps at the age of 52. And that's what the radical middle needs to tell the American people.

RESOURCES

Texts

For recent proposals for a universal draft permitting draftees to choose between military and civilian service, see Amitai Etzioni, *The Spirit of Community* (1993), 113–15; Robin Gerber, "For a New Kind of Draft," *Christian Science Monitor* (13 November 2001); Paul Glastris, "A New Draft for a New Time," *The Responsive Community* (Spring 2002); David Hackworth, "Harry Truman Had It Right," King Features Syndicate (8 September 1999), accessible online; Mickey Kaus, *The End of Equality* (1992), 81–85; Michael Lind, "Citizenship and Sacrifice," *The Responsive Community* (Spring 2002); and Charles Moskos and Paul Glastris, "Now Do You Believe We Need a Draft?" *Washington Monthly* (November 2001).

For interesting variants on the universal draft / free choice of type of service idea, see Marc Magee, "From Selective Service to National

Service," Progressive Policy Institute (2003), accessible online, and Charles Rangel, "Bring Back the Draft," *New York Times* (31 December 2002). For the sad history of President Clinton's National Service Bill, see Steven Waldman, *The Bill* (1995).

Groups

While traditional peace and justice groups sit on their duffs, Brookings Institution (www.brookings.edu) has taken the lead in trying to revive the notion of some form of national service, compulsory or otherwise. See E. J. Dionne, Jr. and Kayla Drogosz, "The Promise of National Service," Brookings Institution (2003), accessible online, and E. J. Dionne, Jr. et al., *United We Serve: National Service and the Future of Citizenship* (2003), a Brookings anthology featuring contributions from over 30 writers and activists.

PART FIVE

HELP THE
DEVELOPING WORLD

13

GLOBALIZATION—
WITH SAVVY AND FEELING

I 'VE BEEN FASCINATED watching friends and acquaintances
respond to globalization—our rapidly dissolving economic (and
cultural, and psychological) borders. At one extreme is Robert.
In his 20s he was a peace activist. In his 30s he earned a joint
J.D./M.B.A. from Columbia, then spent the next decade helping rich
Japanese investors buy up prime U.S. real estate without any troubled feelings whatsoever, so far as I could tell, about the larger implications of his lucrative deal-making (and this at a time when we were
all concerned that Japan might soon be overtaking us as an economic
power).

At the other extreme are the antiglobalists. After the demonstrations in Seattle in 1999, curiosity drew me to Philadelphia for their
next big U.S. bash: the demonstrations during the 2000 Republican
National Convention. Thousands came from across the country, and
I ate with them, slept among them (in some ratty sheets), and talked
and argued with them deep into the night.

Demonstrated with them, too. Even ran with them, up and down
the streets, the day they rioted. I saw one kid wearing
a bandanna over his face jump up and down on the hood of a parked
police car, while another masked guy—a lot closer to my age—shat-
tered the window with a steel rod. I watched peace people overturn
dumpsters and set the contents of one on fire. I watched dozens of
demonstrators laugh and cheer as others spray-painted buses that
were stuck in the rush-hour traffic. They screamed a lot, too: "Whose

streets? Our streets!" "No, no, W.T.O.!" "Come home, America!"
"THIS IS WHAT DEMOCRACY LOOKS LIKE!"

Not a pretty sight. But if you talked with the protesters, you'd
have come away with a better impression of them. Yes, their tactics
were myopic and destructive; and yes, their politics and economics
were as foolish as their tactics suggested (you can fairly call them
neo-anarchist). But beneath it all they were raising real concerns
about the free trade system supporting globalization—concerns that
too many high-achievers like Robert appear oblivious to.

They were ridiculously alienated from mainstream America. But
who wouldn't want to combine their visceral concern for economic
justice—their feeling, their passion—with Robert's sophisticated understanding of economics and savvy about how the world works?

That's what the radical middle is about. As the dust settles from
the first round of protests against globalization, a new perspective on
globalization is arising. It owes much to recent dialogues between
representatives of Washington, D.C., think tanks and representatives
of the antiglobalization movement. And it owes much to not-so-po-
litically-correct nongovernmental organizations (NGOs) like Oxfam
International, which released an influential report in 2002 pronounc-
ing a plague on the houses of both "globophiles" and "globophobes"
and demanding that activists stop "romanticizing poverty" by promoting no-growth or self-reliance scenarios for the third world.

Helping other peoples is one of the Four Key Values of the radical middle. Because globalization is so ubiquitous now (and potentially so promising), we can't help other peoples if we don't do
globalization right. A radical middle approach to globalization would
speak to each of the five issues that—as I learned in the streets—are
of most concern to antiglobalist demonstrators. But it would speak to
them without abandoning mainstream economics and without assuming that caring people can't make our institutions work for decent ends.

TAKING JOBS AWAY FROM AMERICAN WORKERS?

The protesters are convinced that world trade is taking jobs away from
American workers. So is John Sweeney, president of the AFL-CIO—
that's why so many union members turned out in Seattle and Philly.

The protesters are partly right. Some kinds of jobs are disappearing. But that's not the whole story. First, most jobs are disappearing because of technological change (or the normal ups and downs of the business cycle), not because of trade. According to Ed Gresser of the Progressive Policy Institute, an arguably radical middle think tank, trade may account for as little as 5 percent of total job loss in the U.S. Trade just happens to be a convenient scapegoat for politicians.

Another key point is that, overall, the U.S. has added tens of millions of new jobs since globalization began in earnest. As a percentage of national output, the sum of imports and exports rose from 9 percent in 1960 to over 25 percent by the late 1990s. But the fraction of working-age Americans with jobs has grown—from 55 percent in 1950 to 64 percent by the late 1990s.

Some Americans have lost their jobs—especially traditional manufacturing jobs—as a result of the efforts and achievements of foreign producers. But different jobs have been created in other sectors of the economy, and most of those jobs are good jobs. About 80 percent of today's jobs can be classified as service jobs. But more than two-thirds of those are what futurist David Snyder calls "producer-service" jobs—in marketing and sales, information systems management, research and development, and the like. Only about one-fourth of service jobs are what Snyder calls "consumer-service" jobs—short-order cook, bellman, taxi driver, and the like.

We still have an extraordinarily robust and creative economy. In services, burgeoning fields include real estate, transport, finance, health care, and business services. Even in manufacturing we're among the world's leaders in motor vehicles, aerospace, telecommunications, chemicals, electronics, and computers.

One reason we're doing well in these areas is other nations want our products. Few Americans realize we export roughly one-quarter of the $2.7 trillion in manufactured goods we produce each year. Service industries export less, but the fastest-growing export sector of all now is services—financial services, telecom, distribution, professions, software, and entertainment.

If the protesters were less viscerally anti-capitalist, and more open to mainstream economics, they'd see that nations import goods and services not because of a capitalist conspiracy to stab working people in the back, but because other countries are better able to produce certain goods more cheaply (think cotton clothing from India or China) or because of the superior workmanship of foreign competitors (think VCRs from Japan). Even if we were superior at everything, we'd still gain by specializing—just as a doctor who's a terrific typist gains by specializing in seeing patients and hiring an assistant to do her record keeping.

So in the long run, it's in everybody's interest to let the globalization process go forward. Other countries, including poor countries, can find a market here for their products. That can make them better off. Meanwhile, we can specialize in sophisticated and potentially more lucrative fields—aerospace, telecom, and the like. On the whole, better jobs will be created for U.S. workers than the ones that are lost. And U.S. workers will also benefit by being able to purchase the cheaper or better-crafted foreign products. Finally, the economy itself will benefit because competition from imports can increase the efficiency and quality of domestically produced goods—hold down price increases—and generally restrain inflation.

So our problem is not globalization. The problem, and it's very real, is that the workers whose jobs are being lost often can't fit easily into the new kinds of jobs that are being created—basically high-tech manufacturing jobs, professional jobs, and producer-service jobs. These jobs are often higher-paying and higher-status. But many industrial workers lack the training and education necessary to succeed at them. So they end up drifting into low-end manufacturing and low-end service jobs, and paying a huge financial (and psychological) price.

The "globaphiles"—to use Oxfam's language—could care less. To them life wouldn't be life without winners and losers. The "globaphobes," including the protesters, would stop or severely restrict globalization. Those of us at the radical middle welcome globalization—but we insist that the transition to a fully globalized economy be as humane as anything this country has ever done.

That means every worker displaced by trade or technology should get all the help they need in order to move on to some other, comparably rewarding job. Three measures might be particularly helpful:

free access to top-of-the-line job training programs; moving allowances (if the worker chooses to move); and two-year, 50 percent wage supplements. For example, if a worker is displaced from a $2,000-a-month job and takes a stop-gap, $1,000-a-month job, he or she would be provided with a 50 percent wage supplement ($500 a month) for up to two years—long enough to complete a training program and find a better job.

With programs like these, plus the other measures advocated in this book, the transition to a fully globalized U.S. economy should go smoothly.

HURTING THE AMERICAN CONSUMER?

Many protesters in Philadelphia insisted to me that globalization is hurting the American consumer. That goes beyond ignoring mainstream economics, it turns it upside down.

It's understandable though. The job losses suffered by workers in the auto, apparel, and shoemaking industries are constantly in the news. But many of the benefits enjoyed by all Americans as a result of free trade are often either invisible or taken for granted.

Cars, clothes, and shoes are cheaper, better made, or more varied because of free trade. One-fourth of our manufacturing income depends on our ability to export. Every worker with a pension fund benefits by the fund's ability to invest abroad. Every person with a home mortgage or car loan pays less interest because of America's attractiveness to foreigners as a place to invest their money.

Think of protectionism (tariffs or subsidies) as an invisible tax on consumers—a tax to protect old-style manufacturing and farming jobs—and you'll get a true sense of what failure to move to a free trade regime is costing us. Trade restrictions work just like taxes, since products like food, clothing, and appliances are more expensive when they face tariffs or receive subsidies. Alex Greenbaum of the New America Foundation, our first explicitly radical centrist think tank, claims that the average American taxpayer will pay more than $600 a year extra because of the increases in the recent farm bill alone.

By contrast, look at what free trade agreements can do for the American consumer (including cash-strapped workers). According to U.S. Trade Representative Robert Zoellick, the two key agreements of the 1990s—NAFTA and the Uruguay Round—have lowered the cost of purchases for an average family of four by at least $1,300 a year. And if we let the developing countries have their way in the World Trade Organization, even bigger savings could be had by all.

Lowering barriers to foreign goods and services delivers the equivalent of a tax cut to every American consumer.

INCREASING GLOBAL POVERTY?

The protesters are convinced that globalization is increasing global poverty. Actually, it's not at all certain that global poverty is increasing. Many economists claim that the widening income gap between rich and poor countries is due to rising incomes at the top, not falling incomes at the bottom. There's also the inconvenient (for antiglobalists) recent World Bank study which found that per-capita income in globalizing developing countries grew more than 5 percent a year during the 1990s—while for non-globalizing countries, it fell by over 1 percent a year.

Radical middle thinkers and activists shouldn't overstate the world's problems. But it's morally obtuse to come across as some Washington, D.C. think tanks and policy analysts do and reduce everything to statistics. Much of the world is grim and unhappy, and our task is to make it better.

Probably the biggest single thing we can do to end global poverty is to end all tariffs and quotas on exports to the U.S. from the poorest nations. Hopefully we could shame the European Union into following suit—if anything, its barriers to exports from poor nations are slightly higher.

One of the saddest and least-known facts in today's world is that North American and European governments' most restrictive trade barriers are not directed at each others' products, but at products from the poorest nations, such as cotton goods from Africa and agricultural products from Latin America. According to a study by Joseph Francois of Erasmus University in the Netherlands, trade restrictions in the rich countries of the North cost developing countries a minimum of $90 billion a year. That's twice as much as they receive in aid, and many times what they'll ever receive in grants from every capitalist exemplar of "social responsibility."

Another important step toward reducing world poverty would be to drastically reduce subsidies to U.S. and European agribusinesses, now exceeding $300 billion (yes, billion) a year. The subsidies make it possible for "us"—that is, our big farmers and ranchers—to undercut the prices of crops from poor countries both at home and abroad. Few things could be more devastating to poor countries' attempts to earn capital abroad. And, of course, few things could generate more cynicism in the developing world about our real commitment to free trade and globalization. It was the wealthy nations' refusal to offer sufficient compromises on agricultural subsidies that led to the walkout of African, Asian, and Latin American delegates at the WTO talks in Mexico in 2003. Antiglobalists picketing the talks claimed victory—but it was not the kind of victory a radical middle person would care to crow about.

It's important to note that the WTO and other international agencies don't actually write the trade rules. Self-centered and shortsighted governments hammer them out at the WTO and elsewhere . . . most of them democracies, and most of them in constant consultation with interest groups back home. That's not something the far right or far left wants to fess up to. But it's something the radical middle insists on coming back to again and again. If we want to help poor nations, we have to focus on the long-term benefits of free trade for the U.S. and the poor nations alike, meanwhile dealing in a caring way with the negative effects of globalization on certain sectors of the U.S. economy.

DRIVING DOWN LABOR AND ENVIRONMENTAL STANDARDS?

Many protesters in Philadelphia insisted to me that U.S. companies abroad were hurting living conditions in the developing countries. In its book *Whose Trade Organization?: Corporate Globalization and the Erosion of Democracy*, the group Public Citizen captures the mood when it says, "Commerce takes precedence over everything."

Nice rhetoric, poor analysis. The evidence shows that, on the whole, free trade improves labor and environmental standards. Multinationals usually pay higher-than-average wages in developing countries in order to recruit better workers. And they often favor higher regulatory standards than the local competition—if only because they know local firms will have a harder time satisfying them.

The "race to the bottom" in labor and environmental standards is largely a myth. Only 4 percent of U.S. investment abroad goes to production facilities in poor countries that exploit local resources and export back to the U.S. The vast majority of U.S. investment is directed toward countries with relatively strict labor and environmental standards—not for humanitarian reasons, but to tap into those countries' developed or developing markets. Thanks to their increasingly appealing markets, nations as diverse as Brazil, India, and China are perfectly capable of regulating corporate suitors. It isn't trade that wreaks havoc on workers and the environment, it's inept or corrupt governments and the corporations that take advantage of them.

What's frustrating to those of us at the radical middle isn't globalization; it's that the wonderful possibilities inherent in globalization have hardly been tapped.

We shouldn't be telling developing nations to starve social services and waste the environment for 50 to 100 years while they build up a prosperous and environmentally conscious middle class. The world has changed dramatically since the U.S. slowly built up its financial and human capital, and we're all a lot wiser now, and a lot more closely connected. We should be offering developing nations aid—or, better yet, unrestricted access to our markets—in exchange for having them progressively raise their labor, environmental, human rights, and (most important of all, perhaps) educational standards.

We might also want to create a Global Environmental Organization (GEO), as Yale environmental scientist Daniel Esty has been urging for years, and then have it and the International Labor Organization (ILO) create specific environmental and labor standards for multinational firms to meet.

Both the GEO and ILO could then issue periodic "report cards" on firms, and we could use those reports in two ways. We could insist that all multinationals put their labor and environmental "letter grades" onto all their consumer products. The outcry should awaken public interest in firms' performance! We could also—and simultaneously—exempt U.S. multinationals from all taxes on their worldwide income. But we should condition the exemption on their earning respectable grades from the ILO and GEO.

LOSING OUR SOVEREIGNTY TO AN UNDEMOCRATIC WTO?

The protesters I met enjoyed nothing better than bashing the World Trade Organization, and the antiglobalist literature is obsessed by this. Jerry Mander, president of the International Forum on Globalization (and best known as author of a book advocating the abolition of television), speaks menacingly of the WTO's "ability to strike down the domestic laws . . . of its member nations," and some NGOs are outraged that NGOs don't get to participate in the WTO's trade talks.

Talk about making a mountain out of a molehill. The WTO isn't taking one snippet of our sovereignty. It is an arbitration mechanism, no more, no less; it takes up issues that governments want it to take up. And it's relatively successful—there's the rub. It is one of the world's first arguably successful efforts to force countries to sit down and hammer out their differences. (No wonder nobody loves the WTO but international lawyers and other globally oriented idealists.) Even so-called binding decisions by the WTO's dispute settlement panel give nations three options—modify the trade regulations in question, compensate the complaining parties, or face retaliation in the form of increased tariffs on exports. We're a long way from international police forces flying in on black helicopters here.

And everybody outside the antiglobalist movement knows it. That's why 146 nations are part of the WTO now, and about 20 more are eagerly waiting to get in.

Still, the WTO is a long way from what it could and should be. First and foremost, it should be made more transparent. All dispute panels should conduct their hearings in public—just like regular court hearings. And all briefs and other written statements should be made public. You're never going to win the public over to free trade if there's no confidence that the proper facts are on the table and the rules are being applied fairly.

Second, the WTO should be more responsive to civil society. Most WTO governments are democracies, so it's absurd to suggest that NGOs should have a seat at the negotiating table. (Why not give corporations a seat too? Or the tens of millions of consumers who shop at Wal-Mart because of its one-stop convenience and low prices?) But it's equally absurd to keep informed and passionate voices out of the dispute resolution process, especially if your goal is to build a truly global village. NGOs, corporations, unions, and other entities should be allowed—even encouraged—to share their thoughts with dispute panels on any issue, in writing, just as groups are permitted to submit amicus curiae briefs to U.S. courts. The only condition: all groups submitting papers to the WTO should have to share them with the press and public, along with detailed information about their control structures and funding sources.

NEW ALIENATION, NEW NATIONALISM— OR NEW CONNECTEDNESS?

The antiglobalization movement is offering us a New Alienation—a conviction that the modern world is Bad. It can be fun to think that way. But I've already lived through the political alienation of the late Sixties and Seventies, and the price isn't worth it. Too much self-denial, too many underemployed 50somethings, too many resentment-tinged souls.

The political right is offering a New Nationalism that's akin to the old selfishness, aptly summed up in Pat Buchanan's unabashed, America-first, "foreigner"-bashing attacks on free trade. Not only has President Bush rejected that siren song, so have most Fortune 500 executives and business school professors. In 2002, Bush backtracked and imposed heavy tariffs on imported steel—not to help the U.S. in the long term, but to help him win friends in Pennsylvania and West Virginia, two states crucial for his reelection. Alas for Bush, by late 2003 it was clear that the tariffs had cost more jobs than they saved, by driving up costs for automakers and hundreds of small machine-tool and metal stamping shops across the Midwest and upper South.

The steel tariff fiasco nicely illustrates the point of this chapter: in the 21st century, free trade and social justice go together, or should be made to go together. With its commitment to free trade and social justice, the radical middle is offering a New Connectedness to all the world's peoples. In addition, with its commitment to working from within mainstream economics and mainstream national and global institutions, the radical middle is offering a plain old connectedness to the everyday world. I think it's the wisest place to be.

RESOURCES

Texts

For radical middle overviews of globalization in general, see Walter Truett Anderson, *All Connected Now* (2001), and Anthony Giddens, "Taking Globalization Seriously," chap. 5 in *The Third Way and Its Critics* (2000). For arguably radical middle overviews of economic globalization, see Gary Burtless et al., *Globaphobia: Confronting Fears about Open Trade* (1998), accessible online; Thomas Friedman, *The Lexus and the Olive Tree*, rev. ed. (2000); and Kevin Watkins, "Rigged Rules and Double Standards," Oxfam International (2002), accessible online.

For direct or indirect responses to critics of globalization, see Jenny Bates, "International Trade and Labor Standards," Progressive Policy Institute (2000); Daniel Esty, "Bridging the Trade-Environment Divide," *Journal of Economic Perspectives* (Summer 2001); Gary Hufbauer, "World Trade After Seattle," Institute for International Economics (1999); Robert Litan, "Moving Toward an Open World Economy," Brookings Institution (1999); and Bruce Stokes, "The Protectionist Myth," *Foreign Policy* (Winter 1999-2000). All are accessible online.

Groups

Organizations taking a radical middle approach to economic globalization include Brookings Institution (www.brookings.edu), Global Economic Policy Program of New America Foundation (www.newamerica.net), Institute for International Economics (www.iie.com), and Project on Trade and Global Markets of Progressive Policy Institute (www.ppionline.org). Organizations trying to make globalization work include Transparency International (www.transparency.org) and U.N. Global Compact Initiative (www.unglobalcompact.org).

14

HUMANITARIAN MILITARY INTERVENTION: NO MORE RWANDAS!

I 'VE ATTENDED MOST OF THE PROTESTS in Washington, D.C. against the war in Iraq, but I've always left early, with a sinking feeling in my stomach.

I'm glad we took Saddam Hussein out; so are most Iraqis. But to have engaged in military intervention without more of the world at our side—and without sufficient post-invasion planning, involving every faction of the Iraqi people—was unforgivable.

The protesters, though, or at least their leaders, aren't concerned with helping America do good in the world. If you sit through their speeches (and you can often catch them, now, on C-SPAN), what you'll hear is paranoid rants against the Bush Administration coupled with irresponsible, demagogic calls to Bring the Troops Home Now.

Just as disconcerting is the wooden, socialist-pacifist rhetoric of many of the speakers. And the obsession with race and ethnicity— you'd think we were living in Bosnia. And the ubiquitous Israel-bashing sliding into Jew-baiting—the most common placard at our last demonstration was "Free Palestine!" Guaranteed to send a chill up every Jewish person's spine.

I don't mean to get on too high of a horse here. One reason I like to hold onto friends from the Sixties and Seventies is they never fail to remind me of my own embarrassing mistakes. For example, after the first big anti-Vietnam war demo in Washington D.C., in April 1965, I was so upset at the moderate tone that I helped organize an angry sit-in the next day in front of the White House. It turned into a media freak show—instead of communicating rational arguments against the war, what we really managed to convey was our beatnik lifestyles, our anti-achievement ethic, and our sympathy for Communist revolution.

So I plead guilty to having committed numerous sins that a new generation of peace activists is committing (and some from my generation are still committing). I am not a perfect messenger. But I'm perfectly positioned to say this much: our movement has learned precious little since the Sixties.

A PEACE MOVEMENT FOR THE 'OOS

How much did the radical peace movement of the Sixties contribute to ending the Vietnam war? Even now, four decades later, it's hard to know. (We tend to forget that the movement lost much of its force by 1969–70, at the very pinnacle of the war.) What is clear to me, though, is that nothing like that movement's pacifist sensibility or an-archo-socialist politics is needed in pursuit of peace today. These days, a tougher and more grounded approach is called for—and radical middle thinkers and activists are at the forefront of articulating it.

One of the radical middle's Four Key Values is help other peoples. And it is not helpful to other peoples to leave them at the mercy of genocidal governments or movements and call that "peace."

Since the fall of the Berlin Wall in 1989, over six million people have been killed in unimaginably savage ethnic conflicts. Over 12 million more have been wounded or maimed. At least 35 million have been turned into refugees.

Among caring people around the world, there's a haunting sense that we have an obligation as human beings to stop the slaughter of innocents—and help create stable social and economic environments—in places like Somalia, Bosnia, the Sudan, Haiti, Rwanda, Kosovo, Congo, East Timor, Sierra Leone, Iraq, Israel-Palestine, and Liberia.

Even if that means taking up arms.

Because of this emerging new sense of obligation—at once pragmatic and moral—an utterly new kind of "peace movement" is called for today.

The Old Peace Movement raged against injustice in the world with slogans like "Yankee Go Home!" That movement is still with us in the form of the street protests against the war in Iraq, and in pacifist-socialist peace groups ranging from International ANSWER to Peace Action.

The emerging New Peace Movement doesn't have Yankee Imperialism to blame for the murderous ethnic and civil conflicts flaring up all over the world. If radical middle groups like Fund for Peace and Search for Common Ground recognize an enemy at all, it's a more tragic enemy—prejudice, ignorance, intolerance, disrespect for human rights.

Hence the solution isn't to rail against the Bad Guys or attack traditional values in front of the White House. It's to urge the world to take responsibility for stopping the killings and for bringing life-giving order to countries where order has broken down.

The Old Peace Movement disavowed use of the gun. Our emerging New Peace Movement must learn—is learning—when to call on the world to pick up the gun and intervene in the affairs of sovereign nations.

Obviously, it's best to stop a conflict before it starts, and one aspect of our new movement is its enthusiastic support for what's often called "preventive action"—early public warnings by NGOs and private sector groups; private and public attempts to encourage dialogue and create intergroup empathy and understanding; "preventive diplomacy" by official diplomats or experienced and presumably wise citizens; trade inducements; economic sanctions; and similar measures.

But only humanitarian military intervention can protect the innocent once a conflict starts, and no society can rebuild itself without a modicum of physical security. That's why our new movement's immediate task consists of building public support for armed peacekeeping and peace enforcement missions by international institutions, or regional alliances, or coalitions of the willing.

That task is formidable, to say the least. Our adventure in Iraq won't win new friends for humanitarian military intervention—however poorly planned we can show it to have been. And many on the left and right are almost religiously opposed to intervention.

On the right, scholars at think tanks like the Heritage Foundation want us to stick to our "vital national interests" and not worry overmuch about suffering in the world. On the left, magazines like *The Nation* tend to see even Democrat-led attempts at humanitarian military intervention as Vietnam redux, evidence of a sinister plot to dominate the world. Even the Pentagon is unhappy with the new interventionism. According to National Book Award-winning journalist Bob Shacochis, many in the Pentagon see it as somehow beneath us, a kind of "babysitting" that only sissified second-tier countries like Canada and Sweden should be doing.

But beneath the drumbeat of all the naysayers, a powerful case for a new peace movement can be and is being made. . . .

WHY INTERVENE?

There are two kinds of reasons—pragmatic and moral—for the international community to involve itself in ethnic and civil wars.

First and foremost are the moral. How can we stand by and watch millions of innocent people be slaughtered just because they have the wrong skin color or ethnic background? It's not like the international community doesn't have, collectively, the experience and the resources and the means to stop at least some of the killing.

I don't mean to minimize the difficulties. For example, everyone remembers the "Black Hawk Down" incident in October 1993, when eighteen U.S. soldiers were killed during a firefight in Somalia. But few of us remember what was going on in Somalia: the government had essentially collapsed, hundreds of thousands of Somalis had died of starvation, and millions more were facing the prospect of starvation. The U.N. had stepped in. But rival armies and bands were keeping food and other relief services from getting to the destitute Somalis.

In response, the U.S. began helping to get food and supplies through. It was one of our noblest actions since the Marshall Plan. Unfortunately, we didn't stop there. We also began going after individual rebel leaders. Had we stuck with the U.N.'s original game plan, the Black Hawk Down incident would never have happened—and peace might have been brokered a lot sooner than it eventually was.

On the whole, our participation in Somalia was a good thing. Thanks to U.S. troops working in concert with the U.N., massive amounts of food and medicine were delivered to the Somali people. Hundreds of thousands of lives were saved.

And partly because of lessons learned from that experience, some later interventions came off more smoothly. For example, in 2003, soldiers from several West African countries—backed up by a small but phenomenally competent contingent of U.S. Marines—entered Liberia and ended a brutal 14-year war. A U.N. peacekeeping force entered Liberia shortly thereafter.

Why weren't those Marines hailed in this country as global heroes? Our emerging new peace movement should make that sort of thing one of its first orders of business.

Most Americans don't have to be sold on the morality of humanitarian military intervention. According to the nonpartisan Program on International Policy Attitudes at the University of Maryland, over 75 percent of us believe that in principle "there are some times when other countries have the right to intervene to protect people from their own government." According to the respected Pew Research Center, most of us support the continued deployment of U.S. forces in the Balkans, and most of us favor military intervention to prevent genocide in Africa.

Of course, you don't hear that sentiment much from our leaders in Congress. But if you search hard enough, you can. For example, in 2001 Reps. Jim McGovern (D-Mass.) and Amo Houghton (R-N.Y.) introduced a bill that would have had the U.S. urge the U.N. to establish a permanent standing "rapid deployment force" of 6,000 volunteers from all over the world. Although the bill went nowhere, it managed to pick up 55 co-sponsors—including 10 of the 17 House members that my newsletter designated as radical middle.

The second highest-ranking House Democrat—Rep. Steny Hoyer (Md.)—is also on our moral wavelength. "Americans want to do good," he told an audience at the Woodrow Wilson Center, a leading Washington, D.C., think tank, in a speech that generated little publicity. "They want their foreign policy to have a moral and idealistic component. . . . Genocide and mass slaughter debases our nation's principles and insults our collective conscience, whether it occurs in Kosovo, Rwanda, or East Timor. . . . As the world's one military and economic superpower, we have the opportunity—and in my view, the responsibility—to promote an international moral order."

A deeper moral argument for the New Peace Movement is that we have a vital human need to struggle against what political philosopher Michael Ignatieff calls the "culture of death." In other words, we need to uphold whatever it is that distinguishes people from beasts. For the sake of our own humanity, we can't be allowed to descend to a level where people—usually 12- to 30-year-olds—routinely run around hacking each other to death for power or money or status. Otherwise it seeps into the very definition of who we are.

The pragmatic arguments for humanitarian military intervention are equally strong, and probably at least equally compelling for most Americans.

There is, first and foremost, the undeniable fact that failure to respond to global atrocities would weaken our moral authority and our international legitimacy as a global leader.

Then there's the fact that military intervention can make a huge difference in terms of saving lives and restoring civilian order. Everybody knows this, but we need to say it loudly and often. No one's said it more loudly or to more powerful effect than General Romeo Dallaire, the former commander of the straitjacketed and inadequately prepared U.N. forces in Rwanda. Over a span of about 100 days in 1994, Hutu militants slaughtered about 800,000 moderate Hutus and ethnic Tutsi—many with machetes. And the world did essentially nothing.

General Dallaire has repeatedly said that with 5,000 combat-ready troops and the right mandate, he could have saved about half a million lives. Many investigators have backed him up over the years, including prize-winning author Philip Gourevitch and the careful scholars at the Carnegie Commission on Preventing Deadly Conflict.

Another pragmatic argument I like—and many conservatives like, too—is that too much disorder in other countries is bound to lead to an explosion later on. Better peace in a context of international enforcement of justice than no peace, no justice, and no secure investment opportunities.

- Is there a high probability that the intervention will make a sustainable difference, one that would change things in the long term for the better?
- Would the intervention run the risk of triggering a larger war?
- What other consequences might the intervention have?
- What would be the probable results of other policies?
- What would be the probable results of doing nothing? Could you sleep soundly at night?

If we'd asked ourselves these questions in 1994, we'd have surely urged the U.N. to take stronger and swifter action in Rwanda. Even the question about our national interests might have been answered in the positive—acceding to the slaughter lowered our standing in all Africans' eyes and helped destabilize other nations in the region.

HOW TO INTERVENE

No radical middle thinker or activist wants the U.S. to go it alone. But few of us think the U.N. could be the sole player most of the time, either. Military intervention—peace enforcement in the midst of turmoil, as distinct from purely preventive peacekeeping—has never been its strong suit. And the Security Council, which is supposed to make peace-and-security decisions under the U.N. Charter, is hardly representative of today's global community.

Even Kofi Annan is uncomfortable with the Security Council as it is today. He thinks it takes too long to reach decisions, and he wants to make it more representative—which might actually help it move more decisively. Most obviously, the Security Council should be enlarged. Now there are only five "permanent members"—the U.S., Great Britain, France, Russia, and China. Like many other radical middle thinkers, I'd boost it to 12–15 members, taking geography, population, gross domestic product, and level of international engagement into account.

With a more vigorous Security Council, the U.N. might authorize humanitarian armed interventions more speedily and more often. But even then a lot of the responsibility for carrying them out is going to have to remain on the shoulders of regional or subregional organizations, or coalitions of the willing, or a "lead country" in the region in question (for example, Nigeria in West Africa). As Brookings Institution's radical middle military analyst Michael O'Hanlon points out, smaller-scale, decentralized entities are usually better intervenors since they're generally more competent, more meritocratic, better informed, more flexible, and more immediately vested in the outcome.

It would also help if the U.N. had a better pool of soldiers to draw upon. Instead of setting up a permanent U.N. military force, as international law professor Saul Mendlovitz and others have suggested, O'Hanlon wants the U.N. to develop the capacity to quickly "borrow" up to 200,000 specially trained security personnel from nations around the world for specific military interventions. (Up to 40,000 of those would be police officers—one thing sorely missing in post-invasion Iraq.)

And that suits the radical middle just fine. We don't dream of a centralized, one-world government with its own army. We embrace the world's complexity and are perfectly comfortable with decisions being made and carried out by many actors at many levels, with coordination at the top. We've even coined a term for this: "global governance."

WHAT TOMORROW MAY BRING

In the Sixties, the quasi-pacifist peace movement fostered certain qualities in its followers—gentleness, irony, self-sacrifice, anarchosocialist rhetoric, alienation from the System. At the time, it was what the world needed. Or what those of us who put our bodies on the line thought it needed.

In the 21st century, a radical middle peace movement calling for humanitarian military intervention will undoubtedly foster qualities appropriate to it. Physical courage. A love of moral, practical, and legal reasoning. A commitment to working for change within the System. A willingness to think constructively about military sources and forces. A certain gravitas.

I can hardly wait.

RESOURCES

Texts

For pragmatic radical middle rationales for humanitarian military intervention, see Kofi Annan, "Intervention," Ditchley Foundation Lecture (26 June 1998); Scott Feil, "Preventing Genocide: How the Early Use of Force Might Have Succeeded in Rwanda" (1998); and Rep. Steny Hoyer, "Military Intervention for Humanitarian Purposes," speech at Woodrow Wilson International Center (18 September 1999). All are accessible online. For more philosophically rich radical middle rationales, see Michael Ignatieff, *The Warrior's Honor* (1998), and Samantha Power, *"A Problem from Hell": America and the Age of Genocide* (2002).

For radical middle attempts to lay the groundwork for intervention, see Fund for Peace, "Neighbors on Alert" (2003), accessible online; Michael Glennon, "The New Interventionism: The Search for a Just International Law," *Foreign Affairs* (May-June 1999); Richard Haass, *Intervention* (1999), accessible online; and Michael O'Hanlon, *Expanding Global Military Capacity for Humanitarian Intervention* (2003).

Groups

National organizations broadly supportive of the positions taken here include Carnegie Commission on Preventing Deadly Conflict (www.ccpdc.org) and Regional Responses to Internal War Program of Fund for Peace (www.fundforpeace.org). Organizations wanting to see the U.N. play a more assertive peace-building role include Campaign for U.N. Reform (www.cunr.org), Partnership for Effective Peacekeeping Operations (www.effectivepeacekeeping.org), and U.N. Association of the U.S.A. (www.unausa.org).

15

TOUGH ON TERRORISM—
AND TOUGH ON THE
CAUSES OF TERRORISM

THE WALLS OF MY APARTMENT in center-city D.C. are crammed with what you might expect from reading this book—yellowing photos of my civil rights group from 1964–65, exquisite reproductions of Schiele and Rothko and van Gogh (purchased when I was making a lawyer's salary, sigh), a home-made and constantly amended timeline of 100 civilizations from the last 5,000 years. No one who knows me and sees this stuff is sur-prised by any of it. However, one mundane item rarely fails to throw my visitors for a loop: at the top of each of my windows I've duct-taped some rolled-up plastic sheeting.

I've done this, I invariably tell them, with a particular scenario in mind. After the dirty bomb explodes or any other chemical or biolog-ical attack takes place, I peel off a strip of duct-tape and—voila—the plastic sheeting instantly rolls down to cover the window. Assuming I'm still conscious, I then duct-tape the sides of the plastic sheeting. Each window takes two minutes.

It is fascinating how many people are bothered by this; and—I've got to say it—the more liberal they are, the more they tend to be bothered. Usually I'll respond politely by defining the issue as one of routine social responsibility: what if some horrible attack happened when friends or family were visiting? But I know—and my visitors know—that the issue is deeper than that.

Many good people have a hard time getting it through their heads that, for all our power, we are incredibly vulnerable. And that we have a right, even a duty, to protect ourselves. Thousands of people have trained or are in training to kill us; some are here now on our soil (alleged terrorist cells in Buffalo, Detroit, Seattle, and Portland have recently been broken up). Just because a person believes in social justice doesn't mean that he or she has a moral obligation to act as if the world is kinder than it really is. In fact, if we really want to do good in the world, one of our principal obligations is to make sure that we and other caring people are around to do good.

Still, that's only half the task. If you're at the radical middle, and are committed to helping other peoples, then you know your enemy isn't just trained killers. Thanks to television and the Internet, and incessant global travel, everyone knows what successful societies feel like. And everyone knows what unsuccessful societies feel like. If you're living in an unsuccessful society, you can blame your own government and culture, or you can blame the successful societies—most conspicuously, the U.S. So besides protecting ourselves from Al-Qaeda and its imitators, we'll want to give people in failing states some good reasons to prefer getting their own houses in order to blaming everything on us. Three good reasons are friendship, markets, and economic assistance, which together add up to the best reason of all: hope.

So to deal with terrorism, we need to adopt a two-track strategy. It is important to be tough on terrorism—to recognize that we're involved in a new kind of war, against a new kind of enemy, and that in order to defend ourselves effectively enough to win the war we're going to have to recalibrate the balance between security and privacy and make good use of new detection technologies. But it is also, and equally, important to be tough on the causes of terrorism—to dialogue with Muslims from every walk of life, promote political and social reform in the Muslim world, welcome Muslim exports, develop a Marshall Plan for the world's poor, wean ourselves from dependence on oil, and impose a solution in Israel-Palestine.

Think of terrorism as a kind of cancer. If you have a cancerous lung tumor, you'll want to destroy the tumor. But you'll also want to stop smoking. The first requires difficult action, the second, sacrifice. You'll need to do both in order to get well and stay well.

However obvious that may sound, it is not at all obvious in the polarized world of American politics. The vast majority of bestselling political authors today, from Laura Ingraham and Bill O'Reilly on the right to Molly Ivins and Michael Moore on the left, emphasize either-or: either being tough on terrorism *or* being tough on the causes of terrorism, either the first track *or* the second. It's a great way to score ideological debating points, but a terrible way to get us moving down both tracks at once. Only the radical middle can do that.

TOUGH ON TERRORISM

George W. Bush is right about one thing—war has been declared against us, and we are now at war.

Of course, the way Bush sometimes makes this point, with cowboy theatrics, just muddies the waters. A more radical middle way of putting it is that there's no precedent for the kind of conflict we're in. At the very least, though, non-state actors are staging politically motivated acts of war. And those acts require nation-states to act, for their citizens' own protection, as if they are at war—including treating terrorists as enemy combatants. In that sense, we are at war.

Arguably, the war began on February 26, 1993. That's the day Ramzi Yousef and his friends exploded a truck bomb in New York's World Trade Center, more than eight years before 9/11. "Only" six people were killed. I was in New York at the time—was going to law school—and I remember sitting on top our law school dorm that night with my dorm-mates, looking out at the Twin Towers and arguing over whether the incident was, in one student's words, a "one-shot deal."

I was one of the few who felt it was the harbinger of something big; something that had been brewing in the Muslim world for a long time. Most of my fellow students felt it was simply a law-enforcement matter involving a couple of nuts. Most continued feeling that way even after the trial revealed that Yousef's phenomenally ambitious goal was to topple one tower onto its twin and set off a cloud of cyanide gas, killing hundreds of thousands.

Now we know better.

Because we're at war, we need to redraw the balance between liberty and security. That's not easy.

Some people think we ought to start from a position of "liberty is prime, and safety interests need to justify every encroachment on liberty." But from the radical middle perspective, both are prime. Either liberty or security—without a big dose of the other—is meaningless. "[We] need to balance individual rights with the need to protect the safety and health of the public," says the Communitarian Platform, a document signed by over 100 radical-middle-oriented thinkers and activists.

So privacy and security exist in a state of natural tension, and sometimes security requires compromising privacy. One of those times is now. We simply cannot have terrorists, including their funders and facilitators, operating freely within the United States. The dangers are too great. We should worry less about the personal inconvenience of being wiretapped or searched under the PATRIOT Act, and more about large numbers of Americans being killed in a carefully concocted terrorist assault.

The PATRIOT Act has come in for relentless criticism not just from the ACLU and other civil liberties advocates on the left, but from libertarians on the right. Most of that criticism is overblown, a result of the poisonous animosity—verging on paranoia—that often substitutes for dialogue now in American civic life (but makes for great entertainment). Five quick examples:

- It is not true that an FBI agent can simply walk into a flight school or farm-supply store or library and demand someone's records. The FBI first has to convince a federal judge that the material is relevant to protecting against terrorism or spying. Also, before even getting to that point, the FBI has to go through several levels of review to open an anti-terror investigation.
- It is true that the federal judge would be sitting in a special Foreign Intelligence Surveillance Act court, which is not open to the public (and is right down the street from where I live). But there's a good reason for that. If terrorists knew they were about to be investigated, any investigation would be worthless.
- Under the PATRIOT Act, our Fourth Amendment right to the privacy of records disclosed to third parties is not being violated. It doesn't exist—we have no privacy right to records disclosed to

third parties. That's why in any criminal investigation the government has always been able to seek someone's credit-card receipts or phone records or library records—and we're considerably safer for it. Now the government can do the same thing in terrorism investigations.

- It is true that, under the PATRIOT Act, libraries or other entities can't challenge a court order to reveal records and can't inform the target of the investigation. But thank goodness for that. Under the PATRIOT Act, the government isn't seeking evidence for use in a courtroom. It's trying to uncover a plot—for example, by trying to find out whether some guy it's suspicious of has researched cyanide. You don't want to let him know you're doing that.

- It is true that, under the PATRIOT Act, the FBI can delay notifying a property owner that his property will be or has been searched—if notice would have an "adverse result." In other words, if the target might flee the country or destroy documents or—God forbid—pull off as much of the plot as time allows. But here again, all the PATRIOT Act is doing is allowing terrorism investigators to do what criminal investigators have long been able to do when lives are at stake.

When I was an anti-draft counselor, my phone was tapped. On two occasions I actually heard agents talking at the other end of it (once they were having an eager conversation about some unlucky draft resister about to land at an airport near Pittsburg, Kansas). I resented it. But I also knew that I was in fact a good bet to be in touch with lawbreakers. It never occurred to me that, under the circumstances, I had some absolute right to privacy. Mostly I laughed about it (and, of course, always warned callers about it).

Electronic technology offers a relatively convenient way to increase our security. Although civil liberties groups typically balk at any introduction of security devices, the choice is really between hiring many, many more FBI agents to question and search us (just imagine how pleasant that would be), using high-tech to monitor us, or burying our heads in the sand. Given those choices—which are provided by life, not me—high-tech is the radical middle way.

Fortunately, some of the most exciting advances in the field of high-tech have been in the area of surveillance technology. Three examples:

- Cameras hooked up to computers can now scan crowds and identify people who've been identified as threats to public safety. Before you label these devices Orwellian, consider that the cameras scan only what can be seen in public by any passerby. Consider too that cameras aren't the least bit inclined to racially profile anyone. They do just what we want investigators to do, only they do it infinitely more efficiently and objectively.
- "Radiation imaging" technology can now see under our clothing (perfect at airports). Eventually human eyes won't be needed; agents would get involved only if a scanner sets off an alert. Other surveillance technology can now penetrate homes and cars, but be calibrated to only detect dangerous items such as anthrax or explosives or biological or chemical weapons devices. Most privacy advocates loathe such technologies. At the radical middle, which is more concerned about the real world than the perfect world, these technologies are welcome because they're a lot better than the real-world alternatives—increasingly frequent pat-downs and body cavity searches, increasingly aggressive searches of homes and cars, or doing next to nothing and keeping our fingers crossed.
- "Smart ID cards" can now be implanted with tiny computer chips that hold data. In addition to the data written on the card (photographs, height, weight, eye color), the chips can hold a unique biometric identifier, such as a digital scan of a thumbprint. If you've been stopped by police or if you're getting on an airplane, you'd place your thumb on a scanner—which could instantly verify whether the card is legitimate and whether you're its rightful owner. In addition, the card could be linked to computerized databases full of relevant information. If we all had to carry smart ID cards, terrorists would have a harder time operating. (So would criminal suspects and deadbeat parents.) Americans have traditionally resisted national ID cards, but about 70 percent of those recently polled by the Pew Research

Center said they'd favor a card that would have to be shown to authorities on request. Call it the Mohammad Atta Effect, or the radical-middleization of freedom-loving Americans.

Some of us may be philosophically uncomfortable with a greater emphasis on security. Up to 1 percent of us may actually be affected by the measures above in some more than casual way. But under the regime above, Mohammad Atta's gang might have spent so much time being questioned, or deported and redeported, that it might never have been able to pull off its ghastly deed. It might even have been caught. I can live with that trade-off . . . pun intended. For me, it's just a part of surviving in the 21st century. Something every radical middle person puts at the top of their wish list.

TOUGH ON THE CAUSES OF TERRORISM

For better or worse—and in fact, for better—it's not enough to use differently balanced laws and ingenious technology to keep terrorism away from our shores. We also have to engage ourselves—passionately and constructively—with the rest of the world, and particularly with the underemployed, cynical, or poor people of the world. Beginning (but not ending) with those in the Muslim world.

We should begin modestly, by engaging in a sincere re-examination of our behavior toward the world. I don't mean flagellating ourselves like the political left might want us to do. I mean trying to see ourselves as others see us.

Established radical middle thinkers like Marc Sarkady, the corporate consultant, and Stanley Hoffman, the Harvard political scientist, have called for just such an exercise. "This means reinvigorating our curiosity about the outside world," says Hoffman. "And it means listening carefully to views we might find outrageous, both for the kernel of truth that may be present in them and [to glean] the stark realities—of fear, poverty, hunger, and social hopelessness—that may account for the excesses of such views."

A radical middle President would encourage this as one of his or her first orders of business; there could be "town meetings" from coast to coast. Even now, we can each get started. The Internet is an extraordinary window on the world. If you gravitate more toward books, you might benefit—as I did—from reading Raja Shehadeh's autobiography *Strangers in the House: Coming of Age in Occupied Palestine* (2002). To the extent there's a radical middle in Palestine, Raja is front and center—he's founder of Al Haq, a respected human rights group, and son of the first prominent Palestinian to call for a two-state solution (back in the 1960s). But even gentle, worldly, nuanced Raja is full of resentment and rage at the powers that be, and by the time you finish this book, you'll be too.

For even tougher stuff, try Pakistani-British activist Tariq Ali's *The Clash of Fundamentalisms*, an impassioned attempt to explain— as the author puts it—"why much of the world doesn't see the [American] Empire as 'good.'"

Next, we should promote dialogues and exchanges between ourselves and the Muslim world. There should be more people-to-people contacts, student exchanges, exchanges of journalists. The group Search for Common Ground once brought an American wrestling team to Iran—that's the spirit! Many more of our professors should teach in universities in the Middle East, and many more of their professors should be invited to teach and lecture here.

It is a myth that there are no moderates in the Middle East, or that all moderates are simply wealthy pro-Westerners. There are many interpretations of Islam at odds with bin Laden's, and there are many examples of Arabs speaking out honestly on the need for social, political, and economic reform—the most prominent recent example being the U.N. document *Arab Human Development Report 2002*, prepared by Egyptian public intellectual Nader Fergany in consultation with over 50 thinkers and activists from across the Middle East. It is incumbent on us to strengthen the hand of these people in every way we can. The most direct way is by helping to fund moderate Muslim scholars and organizations, something most Arab governments are not rushing to do.

We should also encourage, bribe, shame—whatever peaceful means it takes—Muslim nations to begin the tasks of political and social reform. One possibility, recently suggested by France's great radical middle philosopher, Bernard-Henri Lévy, as well as by Brookings Institution's Richard Haass, is to tie foreign aid to certain very concrete goals: permit freedom of the press and you get X, establish schools that don't teach hatred of the West and you get Y, educate girls and young women and you get Z. . . .

Two huge steps—freeing ourselves of dependence on foreign oil, and welcoming Muslim exports—are implicit from earlier chapters of this book. By becoming self-sufficient in energy, we'll be freer to press Muslim countries for reforms. And by opening our markets to Muslim exports, we'll permit more capital to flow to Muslim shores than we'd ever be able to deliver in foreign aid. Ironically, we impose our highest trade barriers on exports that are most important to poor countries, such as clothing and agricultural products. All goods from Muslim countries (including shoes, clothes, textiles, dates, olive oil, and grains) should receive duty-free and quota-free access to the U.S. market, provided only that cooperation against al-Qaeda and non-support for other terrorist groups is forthcoming.

As for foreign aid, few things could do more to reduce terrorism's appeal than for the United States to stop just talking about compassion and start practicing it in a way that's commensurate with our wealth and expertise.

We should draw up a comprehensive plan to ease the suffering of the world's poor, with specific dollar amounts and target dates. Or we should commit ourselves to helping the U.N. achieve the goals set forth in an extraordinary 2003 report by the U.N. Development Program (UNDP), "Millennium Development Goals: A Compact Among Nations to End Human Poverty."

The report represents the U.N.'s first attempt to craft a radical middle and self-critical development strategy—an "open trading system" is part of the compact, as is better governance on the part of the developing countries. The health, education, and welfare goals set forth in the report are admirably basic, and no radical middle thinker or activist would quarrel with any of them: eradicate extreme poverty and hunger, achieve universal primary education for girls and boys alike, reduce by two-thirds the child mortality rate, reduce by three-quarters the number of women dying in childbirth, and begin to reduce the incidence of AIDS, malaria, and all other major diseases.

UNDP Director Mark Malloch Brown estimates it will cost $75 billion a year for the next 15 years to reach these goals. That's definitely real money. But it's still only about 9 percent of the world's military budget, and only about 19 percent of our own military budget. The United States and the European Union should foot that annual bill. And every water tap, food packet, and classroom should come with an attractive logo saying, "Gift of the People of the United States and the European Union."

Last but not least, we need to take hold of the situation in Israel and Palestine. Nobody else will, or can—not even the Israelis or Palestinians at this point. Israel cannot continue to rule three million Palestinians against their wishes; something's got to give, and soon. The most promising radical middle scenario is for the U.S., in concert with other nations, to push the U.N. to establish a trusteeship for Palestine. A trusteeship with a mandate to build a democratic Palestinian state.

The trustees would take control of Palestinian territories from the Palestinian Authority and hold them in trust for the Palestinian people. They would also take control of the occupied territories from Israel and hold them in trust for the Palestinian people. They would then oversee the establishment—by Palestinians—of democratic political institutions, an independent judiciary, and competent economic institutions.

All this would cost billions of dollars and require a long-term, multinational peacekeeping force. But the world's prosperous countries would be well advised to pay the money and contribute the soldiers. After 9/11, it's unnervingly clear that other scenarios could prove far more costly.

CONSIDER THE OPPORTUNITIES

Our brutal new situation—as prime target in a war by terrorists—presents us with certain opportunities, and it's important to grasp them.

First, it's giving us an opportunity to learn that—just as a caring doctor must make use of both allopathic and alternative medicine—so a caring superpower must make use of both military force and social compassion, high-tech defensive measures and high-touch outreach measures. In the larger scheme of things, duct tape and plastic sheeting are but a tiny step in the right direction. Their symbolic importance pales beside the real work that needs to be done.

Second, the terrorist war is giving us an opportunity to understand that globalization is no longer debatable. It's here—we're all connected now—and we need to learn to make the most of it.

Finally, the terrorist war is giving us an opportunity to learn that doing good in the world—one of the Four Key Values of the radical middle—is in our national self-interest. Promoting political and social reform and economic prosperity in the developing world is no longer a matter of unctuous social responsibility. It is a matter of survival. And it can lead to so much more.

RESOURCES

Texts

For the clearest brief radical middle statement on the balance between our liberty interest and our security interest, see Richard Posner, "Security Versus Civil Liberties," *Atlantic Monthly* (December 2001). For an extended meditation on that balance, see Amitai Etzioni, *The Limits of Privacy* (1999). For a convincing defense of the PATRIOT Act, see Heather Mac Donald, "Straight Talk on Homeland Security," *City Journal* (Summer 2003). For high-tech as the barrier of choice against domestic terrorism, see Shane Ham and Robert Atkinson, "Using Technology to Detect and Prevent Terrorism," Progressive Policy Institute (2002). All but Etzioni are accessible online.

For using trade policy to build goodwill in the Muslim world, see Edward Gresser, "Blank Spot on the Map," Progressive Policy Institute (2003). For using foreign assistance to build goodwill, see Dick Bell and Michael Renner, "A New Marshall Plan?" Worldwatch Institute (9 October 2001), and United Nations Development Program, *Human Development Report 2003: Millennium Development Goals* (2003). For a call for the global community to take charge in Israel-Palestine, see Martin Indyk, "A Trusteeship for Palestine," *Foreign Affairs* (May-June 2003). All these texts are accessible online.

Groups

Communitarian Network (www.gwu.edu/~ccps) would readjust the balance between liberty and security. Search for Common Ground (www.sfcg.org) is outstanding at initiating dialogues in and exchanges with the Muslim world. Groups addressing root causes of terrorism include Basic Education Coalition (www.basiced.org), Carter Center (www.carter-center.org), Global Health Council (www.globalhealth.org), Global Marshall Plan Initiative of Search for Common Ground (www.sfcg.org), Microcredit Summit Campaign (www.microcreditsummit.org), Open Society Institute (www.soros.org), and RESULTS (www.results.org).

PART SIX
BE A PLAYER,
NOT A REBEL

16

YOU CAN HAVE A CAREER AND BE POLITICAL, TOO

ANY CARING PEOPLE of my generation felt they had to choose between having a professional career and doing political work. Gerry, one of my best friends ever, was an extreme example. For all the years we knew each other—even after he became a full-time appellate attorney, with sleek sports car and stunning house in Malibu overlooking the Pacific Ocean—he couldn't spend any time alone with me without confessing how much he "really" wanted to live a more politically committed life. Which for him meant, as he often put it, "manifestos and demonstrations and all the rest of it." But he was afraid any political commitment would cause trouble with clients. One gorgeous afternoon he was in fact shot dead by a client; it had nothing to do with politics though.

Gerry's romantic, all-consuming image of political commitment had been frozen in his brain by the armed takeover by radical black students of a building at Cornell (where he'd gone to school) and by the public image of radical activist Tom Hayden, whom he idolized, even though he felt Hayden wouldn't have given someone like him the time of day, except maybe to ask for money. And Hayden—now nearly 65 years old—is still happily and self-servingly creating that impression. At the Ruckus Camp in Malibu in the summer of 2000, not far from Gerry's old home, Hayden attacked "pragmatists" and even "idealists" for being too cowardly or self-centered to become radicals. And his audience ate it up.

Of course, what Hayden means by radical is some witches' brew of identity politics, socialism, and antiglobalism. Those of us at the radical middle have devised a more appealing political perspective, which I've tried to set forth in this book. And we've devised a more effective strategy than Hayden's call for perpetual rebellion. It's a call for all caring people to become players within the System.

The rest of this book lays out that strategy. In this chapter I'll encourage you to ground yourself in the real world—by going to professional school (if possible), by inserting your beliefs into your workplace (too mundane a task for romantics like Gerry), and by staying informed. In the next chapter I'll encourage you to join local, national, and professional groups and pull them to the radical middle. And in the last chapter I'll encourage you to help reform our political system—in part by running for office.

So the radical middle strategy is not about rebellion. But it dovetails with the lives we actually lead. It is about the long haul, and it's about winning. I like to think even Gerry, co-author of a book called *Winning With Your Lawyer,* would have come round to it eventually.

SEND YOURSELF OR YOUR KIDS
TO PROFESSIONAL SCHOOL

For most of the 20th century, small radical groups were seen as social change incubators. The various socialist and communist parties, the Student Nonviolent Coordinating Committee (SNCC), Students for a Democratic Society (SDS), and a thousand local or regional variants were where it was at, and if you wanted to do serious social change work you'd have felt compelled to make one or more of them the center of your life.

There are still thousands of radical left- (and right-) wing groups out there, arguably more than ever. But we live in a knowledge society now—a world that depends increasingly on professional expertise and special skills. If we want to change *that* world, we'll need to be even more expert and skilled than those who'd defend the status quo.

That's why professional schools, not radical groups, are our social change incubators now.

And radical middle social change agents know it. Many of the most idealistic and dedicated of them have been pouring into our graduate schools, including our great medical, business, and law schools.

And it's not just young people fresh out of college. Increasingly, students in their 30s, 40s, and even older have been doing whatever it takes to get into professional school and become more relevant to the extraordinary new world we've made. According to the U.S. Census Bureau, in the school year 2001–2002 the number of students 35 and older in U.S. graduate and professional schools was an astonishing 1,145,000—34 percent of the total. From 1987 to 1999, the number of grad students over 40 grew by 56 percent.

Part of "whatever it takes" is being able to afford it. On the surface, that looks pretty daunting—some professional schools cost a total of over $100,000 to attend (though some fine state schools charge in-state residents dramatically less, and—psst—it usually takes only one year to qualify as "in-state"). But over the last generation, student loans have become increasingly easy to get. Now, virtually any American citizen can borrow up to $100,000 to attend professional school—and if you actually intend to work in your profession (and if you insist that your lenders put you on 10- or 15-, not 20-or 25-year payback schedules), it's not difficult to pay the money back.

I went to law school at mid-career, and that helped me discover the radical middle as a living, breathing force in our society. At least half the students at New York University School of Law were passionately radical middle in outlook, not least of all the older students.

Kathy was a nurse before law school, then decided she wanted to become more proactive in the health sector. "There's so much to humanize in the practice of medicine," she'd say. John was a religious writer who dreamed of helping society work out a better balance between faith and privacy. William was a veterinarian who dreamed of helping society craft a responsible biotech future.

So many good people have been pouring into professional school that the schools themselves have radically changed. There's still an image out there that the professors are apologists for the status quo and the courses are 20 years behind the times. Nothing could be further from the truth now.

Spurred on by hundreds of thousands of students at the radical middle—caring people who want to succeed in life by doing good—

many professional schools are infinitely more visionary and exciting than ideological groups and magazines ever were:

Compassionate MDs.

Instead of just complaining about our health care system, consider going to medical school.

At least 75 of our 125 medical schools offer courses on alternative medicine now—chiropractic, therapeutic massage, homeopathy, and the like. And the Association of American Medical Colleges (AAMC), an umbrella group representing all 125 medical schools, has formed a task force to promote *more* courses on "nontraditional health care" in the schools. Harvard Medical School's David Eisenberg sees a day when mastery of acupuncture or herbal medicine will be as basic to a good medical education as mastery of biochemistry.

Producing empathic doctors is a special goal of many medical schools today, thanks partly to a 1999 AAMC report calling on medical schools to train doctors to communicate effectively with patients and provide compassionate medical care. Johns Hopkins, for example, sends its medical students into inner-city Baltimore in their first year. They quickly discover where their communication skills are lacking! At the South Carolina College of Medicine, students are given seminars on faith, forgiveness, guilt and shame, prayer, tragedy, and spirituality—all to help them communicate with patients who might be disabled, mentally ill, or dying.

Holistic MBAs.

Instead of just complaining about business, go to business school. You won't feel out of place.

Courses on the environment were taught at only a handful of business schools in 1990; now they're offered at over 100 B-schools. Courses in entrepreneurship have gone up from a grand total of 16 in 1970 to over 400 today. And the number of graduate courses in nonprofit management has jumped from 17 in 1990 to roughly three times that today (with full nonprofit management programs at such trend-setting B-schools as Harvard, Stanford, and Wharton).

Even more important, the traditional business school curriculum is beginning to give way to big-picture thinking. At some schools, traditional subjects like finance, marketing, statistics, and accounting are being repackaged as a series of cross-disciplinary subjects with titles like "Creativity and Critical Thinking." And "designer majors" are the rage. Instead of majoring in finance, marketing, etc., you can major in one segment of the economy—say, health care—and draw from all the relevant business disciplines. Vanderbilt and MIT have designer majors in e-commerce now, and Yale and Michigan have especially delicious-looking designer majors in environmental management.

Visionary JDs.
Instead of just complaining about greedy, lawsuit-hungry lawyers and our forbidding legal system, go to law school. You won't believe your eyes.

In the 1980s, few law schools offered courses on mediation, arbitration, and the like (collectively known as "alternative dispute resolution," or ADR), even though the whole country had begun to long for simpler and less costly forms of justice. Today nearly every one of our 180+ law schools offers courses and clinics in ADR, and some law schools have gone so far as to introduce dispute resolution concepts into all required first-year courses. At the University of Missouri, for example, students taking first-year Torts learn how to negotiate settlements in medical malpractice cases.

Law schools used to be dry-as-dust, but there's probably no better place to stretch your mind now than at law school. Courses exploring the social, political, and philosophical dimensions of the law are multiplying now. The "Socratic method"—where the teacher calls on you at random to recite facts or provide analysis (not just spout opinions)—is guaranteed to turn political trippers into radical middle appreciators of complexity and synthesis.

For years the law schools were almost laughably U.S.-centric; not anymore. Both Harvard and Columbia offer over 40 courses on aspects of international law now, and NYU is pumping $75 million into its effort to transform itself into the world's "first global law school." Even the Mickey Mouse requirement called legal ethics is being transformed, at many law schools, into a course exploring powerful new legal ideals for the 21st century.

To sum up: if you think being a social change agent means selling Americans on socialism or libertarianism, find a radical group to belong to. But if you think being a change agent means being a caring person, acquiring invaluable expertise, and applying it in imaginative ways for the common good, then send your kids to professional school. Or take the plunge and go yourself. Chances are you'll get a great and very marketable education, and you won't have to leave your radical middle values at the door.

It will be hard (rigorous professional training always is), and it won't be cheap. But there's no better way to put yourself in a position to help change the world.

TURN YOUR JOB INTO A VEHICLE FOR SOCIAL CHANGE

So you've earned your professional degree and you have your first job. Or you already have a job that suits you just fine. How can you use it to help bring a radical middle perspective into the world?

An extraordinary number of people have been asking that question lately (in their own words and way), and our triumphs and struggles have spawned two remarkable books, Howard Gardner et. al.'s *Good Work* (2001) and Debra Meyerson's *Tempered Radicals* (2001).

Both books report on the authors' long-term, in-depth studies of people who've tried to bring their essentially radical-middle political values into the workplace. Both are by authors who can be comfortably described as radical middle themselves (Gardner is the father of the notion of "multiple intelligences," emotional, artistic, kinesthetic, etc., not just the IQ-testable kind; Meyerson teaches at Stanford Business School and specializes in nonprofit management and women in business).

Their biggest finding: You are not alone. There's a whole subculture now of radical middle social change agents in corporations, in the professions, and in knowledge work in general. Gardner calls them advocates of "'good work'—work of expert quality that benefits the broader society." Meyerson calls them "tempered radicals"— people who "want to fit in *and* . . . retain what makes them different. They want to rock the boat, and they want to stay in it."

Sometimes events force radical middle change agents to reveal their presence to the world. Dramatic recent examples include the Enron employees who tried to warn their superiors about that company's unsustainable course, and the FBI employees who tried to warn their superiors that possible terrorists weren't being adequately monitored. Enron's Sherron Watkins and the FBI's Coleen Rowley weren't ideological radicals looking to strike—they were ethically driven Americans at the radical middle who refused to stand quietly by while their institutions betrayed the public trust.

But most of the time, radical middle change agents at work are out of the public eye.

So how do they—we—operate? How are more and more of us able to act as radical middle change agents without losing our jobs or our standing at work? If you take all the experiences we poured out to Gardner and Meyerson and whittle them down to ten pieces of advice, you'd come up with something like this:

- Help sustain other people's efforts at work. There's no better way to build support for *your* efforts;
- Go out of your way to address ethical issues in your daily interactions with colleagues;
- Challenge norms in small ways. For example, if you work at a coffeehouse or bookstore, get your manager's permission to refuse to wait on abusive customers. By deviating from an accepted norm, you'll encourage more people to attend to their own value priorities;
- Speak out against the deteriorating values in your occupation or profession, without necessarily making your own institution a target of your critique. In fact, constantly speak up for ("reaffirm") the decent values and principles your institution says it stands for;
- Set up new initiatives that circumvent dysfunctional workplace bureaucracies. For example, rather than arguing endlessly over what pro bono cases your firm should take, set up a special pro bono wing of your firm to handle the cases you think are worthwhile;

- Expand the function of your institution in some logical but humane way. For example, some genetics firms have been induced—by radical middle researchers within them—to devote some small portion of their annual budgets to addressing social and ethical issues arising from the research;
- Work hard to diversify the membership of your institution. Diversity *always* boosts radical middle perspectives, since minorities who want to succeed in the mainstream have got to be both practical and visionary;
- Let people see you rise above your own frustration, humiliation, and anger when working on behalf of your larger ideals. It will inspire them to hang on when the going gets tough;
- Choose your battles within contexts in which there's some chance of accomplishing something. Don't pick fights just to let off steam or to turn yourself into some kind of Noble Victim;
- Establish a support group for like-minded people within your institution.

Do all that (or even some small portion of that) and your work life will not only become more interesting and challenging and rewarding. It will become a seamless part of your political life—and viceversa.

STAY INFORMED

If you want to be a radical middle social change agent at work *or* after hours, then you have to stay informed. There's nothing more off-putting than someone who thinks they have solutions to our social problems, but isn't keeping up with current events or other people's solutions.

Besides, it's fun to read great newspapers and innovative books and articles. One of the things that separates radical middle people from ideologues is we're constantly chasing down new facts and perspectives—and incorporating them into our ways of seeing.

Fortunately, it's never been easier to stay informed about politics and current events. You just have to know where to go and what to avoid.

It is important to keep up with your local community, and some-times the local newspaper or a local television station is the best way to do that. But don't allow yourself to stop there—most newspapers and TV news programs are incredibly superficial. No matter where you live, go onto the Internet and look up our four great general-interest newspapers—the *Washington Post,* the *New York Times,* the *Christian Science Monitor,* and the *Los Angeles Times* (that's how I'd rank them at the moment). Or, if you're so inclined, look up the great British papers—the *Guardian,* the *Independent,* and the *Observer*—and the great British news magazine, *The Economist.*

Figure out which one you prefer. Then make sure to read it for at least 10 minutes a day—every day. (Unless you're a true political junkie, one is enough. They all steal shamelessly from one another, so if you stick with one you won't miss anything.) I do this early in the morning every day with a cup of coffee and some morsel by my side, and it's a delightful part of my day.

Unfortunately, even our best newspapers and news magazines don't adequately convey the breadth of political ideas sloshing around today. For that you'll need political magazines or Web sites. Some of my favorite political magazines—all partly or largely viewable on the Web—are *The Nation* (hard left), *In These Times* (activist left), *The New Republic* (dead center), *The Weekly Standard* (conservative), and *Reason* (libertarian). Some of my favorite pure Web sites are Slate.com (smart left), Andrewsullivan.com (smart right), and Art Levine Confidential. Sometimes I'll just go to www.politicaltheory.info, an extraordinary grab-bag of articles from every conceivable point of view.

At the radical middle, we don't define "politics" narrowly. So you should also keep up with the *New York Times Book Review,* also freely available online. It's only superficially about books; it's actually an ongoing multilogue about who we are, how we live, and what we live for. You can't be a radical middle change agent and absent yourself from that intense Thoreauvian stuff. If you prefer electronic media, stay up for the *Charlie Rose* show on PBS. It's the best talk show on television or radio—the guests are our real cultural, business, and political leaders (or should be), and Rose engages them in unbroken, free-flowing, delightfully intelligent conversations for up to an hour each.

To stay abreast of radical middle ideas, you don't need a special "movement" literature—the ideas are buzzing all around you, and in nearly every source mentioned above. But you'll find an unusually high concentration of them in three popular magazines—the *Atlantic*, *Foreign Policy*, and the *Washington Monthly*—as well as in my own bimonthly newsletter, *Radical Middle*, and in Michael Marien's superb monthly review of political books and articles, *Future Survey*.

Finally, if you'd like to overdose on radical middle ideas (one of the most benign overdoses available today), I suggest you regularly monitor the websites of three think tanks, the New America Foundation, the Progressive Policy Institute, and the Brookings Institution. The first is explicitly radical middle (its founders wrote the book *The Radical Center*); the other two post reams of original papers and articles, and often the most radical middle get the least play in the media, since they can't be easily pigeonholed as left or right.

Absorb some of the material above and you'll be a very effective radical middle spokesperson in school or at work. Just as important, you'll be effective in groups (next chapter) and in the political arena (last chapter).

RESOURCES

Texts

For information about the state of professional schools today, see the articles in *U.S. News & World Report*'s annual booklet, *America's Best Graduate Schools*. I found the booklets dated 2001 and 2000 particularly useful for this chapter. Articles from the current booklet are freely accessible online, and articles from prior booklets are available for a fee.

For insight into how caring people are bringing their values into their work lives, see Howard Gardner et al., *Good Work: When Excellence and Ethics Meet* (2001), and Debra Meyerson, *Tempered Radicals: How People Use Difference to Inspire Change at Work* (2001).

Groups

If you doubt my contention that today's professional schools are hotbeds of thoughtful idealism and informed hope, see the website of the American Medical Student Association (www.amsa.org), and pay special attention to the pages labeled "Community & Public Health," "Global Health," "Health Policy," and "Humanistic Medicine." You might also enjoy following the site's links to issues like "Complementary and Alternative Medicine," "Disparities in Medicine," "Healthy Schools and Medical Students," and "Revitalizing Professionalism." If you doubt my contention that caring people are, increasingly, bringing their values into their work lives, see the website "Transforming Practices: Finding Joy and Satisfaction in the Legal Life" (www.transformingpractices.com).

17

JOIN GROUPS THAT MATTER, AND PUSH THEM TO THE RADICAL MIDDLE

URING THE REAGAN ERA, I knew thousands of people from coast to coast who longed to create a "third way" alternative to the political left and right. I'd met most of them during my nearly two-year-long tour on behalf of my book *New Age Politics*. There was Bob, a project director at the U.S. Congress's Office of Technology Assessment; Jim, one of the original Nader's Raiders who'd just gone off in his own less adversarial direction; George, a human resources consultant for major corporations; Nancy, fabled grassroots networker of the Pacific Northwest; and on and on, an amazing array of talent and energy.

Eventually about 50 of us got together, in a glamorous loft in New York City, to figure how to proceed. We were nearly aglow with great new political ideas. But when it came to getting those ideas onto the American political agenda, we were stumped. We ended up doing what many other groups of activists had done over the prior 20 years—creating a new, national political organization, the New World Alliance, with an office in Washington, D.C., a beleaguered staff (I was the first), and big plans to create—if we could ever find the money—a "Transformational Political Platform" to be constantly revised by members, a series of national New World Forums on the great issues of the day, and, of course, a New World Political Action Committee.

For about three years, many more meetings were held, but little money got raised and few projects got done. Astonishing amounts of energy went down the drain.

In hindsight, what's most striking is the gap between the impressive resumes of the individual Alliance members and the disappointing "achievements" of the Alliance. Yes, part of the Alliance's ineptness probably reflected our own individual failings. But a larger part of the problem, I think, is that our model for social change was out-of-date—a relic of the Sixties and Seventies, when tiny groups and "groupuscles" sprang up to Make the Revolution.

We didn't need to create another small, self-contained political organization. Our "third way" ideas (basically, radical middle ideas) were already beginning to bubble up in many mainstream organizations. What we should have done was create a kind of support group that would have encouraged like-minded people to keep burrowing their way toward the heart of the System.

Radical middle thinkers and activists could use that support group today. (This book aspires to be that support group . . . as much as any book can be one.) But even without a support group, the vast majority of us have figured out that we don't need to create oppositional political groups to make our voices heard.

We are in virtually every significant local, professional, and national group now—that's one of the advantages of being Players not Rebels. In fact, you can't spend an hour in any group meeting these days without hearing dreadful radical rhetoric, stultifying liberal or conservative rhetoric . . . and life-giving radical middle thoughtfulness and passion.

We need to continue doing what we have been doing—joining local, professional, and national groups, and nudging them toward the radical middle.

JOIN A LOCAL GROUP

Don't let anyone tell you local groups are dying out. Some of them may look different from the groups we had before, but they're as numerous and feisty as ever. And as popular—Princeton sociologist Robert Wuthnow claims that four out of ten of us now belong to organized local groups that meet regularly and provide purpose and social support for their members.

Some of these groups are explicitly, or implicitly, political. Besides PTAs there are now PTOs, Parent-Teacher Organizations that aspire to be more flexible and creative. There are probably more neighborhood associations today than ever before.

There are tens of thousands of ad hoc groups addressing local problems. There are over two thousand "community development corporations" (CDCs) engaged in housing and community revitalization. There are phenomenally innovative congregation-based community organizing groups, neighborhood watch groups, and community visioning projects.

The radical middle perspective manifests itself in many ways in local groups. If you'd like to find a local group that's radical middle in spirit—or if you'd like to push your local group in a more radical middle direction—here's what you'll want to pay attention to:

- If a local group wades into hot-button issues with hardened positions, it's not radical middle. But if it tries to resolve community differences in creative new ways to everyone's satisfaction, then it couldn't be more radical middle. The Public Conversations Project, near Boston, specializes in teaching local groups how to initiate constructive conversations and relationships in their communities.

- If a local group is too proud or "militant" or suspicious to work with business or government, then it's not radical middle. But if it cultivates potential supporters among local businesspeople and in city hall (and in the bureaucracy around city hall), as Seattle's network of neighborhood associations began doing in the late 1980s, then it's not only radical middle, it's probably going to be effective.

- If a local group takes volunteers or visitors for granted, or thinks of them as outsiders, or treats them as fodder for the next big campaign, then it's not radical middle. But if a group makes an extra effort to make newcomers feel welcome, and makes it easy for them to take part in the proceedings, and makes sure their work is appreciated, then it's radical middle in the best sense.

The grassroots anti-poverty group RESULTS, founded by my friend Sam Daley-Harris, is famous for this.

- If a local group thinks "group process" is something only bureaucrats or Sixties leftovers pay attention to, then it's not radical middle. But if a group prohibits personal attacks, regularly makes use of a facilitator, encourages open discussion, invites quiet people to speak, and follows a clear and coherent procedure to reach decisions, then it's almost surely radical middle.

- If a local group is a "one-man show," or if consists largely of a few heroic, relentlessly dedicated "incandescent citizens," then it's not radical middle no matter how many radical middle positions it takes on the issues. But if a group takes democracy seriously—defines it as, for instance, the shared work of many imperfect people acting pragmatically to stop bad things and produce good things—then the radical middle will never be far behind.

Got it?

JOIN A PROFESSIONAL ASSOCIATION

Professional associations are increasingly influential in our increasingly knowledge-based, complicated, and globalized society. So one great way to have an impact politically is to get involved in a professional association, and nudge it to the radical middle.

Many people suppose that professional groups are only for credentialed members of a profession. But with a few exceptions, that's not so. Most professional groups welcome associated journalists, policymakers, researchers, and activists, and all of them participate fully—even passionately—in the proceedings.

That's what makes many national meetings of professional associations such a delight to behold and attend. Anyone who's ever attended meetings of the American Medical Association, American Society of International Law, American Political Science Association, American Psychological Association, Society for the Advancement of Socio-economics, World Future Society, or the World History Association—to take just a few examples—knows exactly what I'm talking about.

Professional associations are also great places to meet radical middle allies. Caring people who hope to use their expertise for the common good are front and center at professional associations.

The popular image of professional associations is that they're insufferably staid and Establishment-oriented, but like many popular images, it's out of date. Take that paragon of professional associations, the American Association for the Advancement of Science (AAAS).

Back in the Sixties, the AAAS *was* staid and Establishment-oriented. If you were around then, you probably remember radical students bursting into AAAS meeting rooms shouting obscenities and "Science for the people!" by way of attacking the science community's largely supine role in the Vietnam war.

Today, half those radical students have become perpetual rebels and are off attacking biotech or television or whatever. But the other half have become radical middle players, and their impact on AAAS has been huge. Its Science and Human Rights Program now gives aid and comfort to scientists, teachers, and students in oppressive countries around the world; its Black Churches Initiative helps thousands of U.S. churches do science and math education after school hours; and its Program of Dialogue on Science, Ethics, and Religion is trying to raise issues of values and ethics in every lab and lecture hall.

It isn't just the rebels who've clouded up our image of professional associations. Most media coverage is either nonexistent or superficial. Although 800 media folk attended the millennium AAAS meeting in Washington, D.C. (which attracted over 5,500 scientists, educators, policymakers, and activists from around the world), most reporters did little more than hunt for free food, attend press briefings, and report on glamour sessions like "Space Travel for All" and "The Healthy Side of Eating Chocolate."

Meanwhile, out in the trenches—that is, in poorly air-conditioned conference rooms where the real work of the meeting was taking place—at least 14 panels featured radical middle perspectives on the burning social and ecological issues of the day.

You can find the same quiet omnipresence of radical middle ideas in many professional associations now.

At a recent meeting of the American Political Science Association, panelists passionately debated how to "value nature"; how to establish the rule of law in a globalized world; how to mitigate the importance of group identity in domestic politics; how to bring "moral order" to diverse societies.

At a recent meeting of the World Future Society, prominent futurist Clement Bezold argued that a more holistic approach to health is inevitable, *if* we don't let fear win out. And prominent futurist Graham Molitor argued that genetic engineering and nanotechnology can solve our environmental problems, *if* we carefully monitor their development.

At a recent meeting of the American Society of International Law, Harvard professor Anthony Appiah tried to develop a "global moral framework" based on individual dignity rather than collective need.

In the media and on the street, it often sounds like the extremists are winning the crucial political debates. But in the jam-packed conference rooms of the professional associations—where the debates are actually being held—most of the energy, most of the juice, is with the radical middle.

You should join up and pitch in.

JOIN A NATIONAL CITIZEN GROUP

Another great way to push radical middle ideas forward is by joining a national citizen group (aka nonprofit group, interest group, nongovernmental organization). You can find radical middle perspectives in just about any citizen group now—from Children's Defense Fund to Bull Moose Republicans, from National Urban League to National Taxpayers Union—and even if all you do is send in dues, attend the occasional meeting, and send the occasional deftly worded note to the national office, you'll be helping move your citizen group to the radical middle.

Parts of the left have begun to disparage national citizen groups. For example, Benjamin Barber, who runs the Walt Whitman Center for the Culture and Politics of Democracy at Rutgers University, says citizen groups represent "thin" rather than "thick" democracy since they're not primarily local, face-to-face groups. Theda Skocpol—a Harvard professor—worries that they're "professionally dominated."

National citizen groups are indeed organs of representative not direct democracy. But that's what makes them appealing to people at the radical middle. Because we tend to be heavily committed to our jobs and our personal lives, we don't have time to attend endless local and regional meetings and spend endless hours hammering out "consensus" positions that might very well need to be redrawn the next week. It's not how we choose to live, and it's not how we want American democracy to work. Direct democracy would give disproportionate power to those whom I called (in Chapter Two) "self-sacrificing individuals"—the kind of people who make political struggle the centerpiece of their lives—folks who tend to be found on the far left and far right.

Because national citizen groups are under attack, some thinkers at the radical middle have sprung to their defense. Heart of their case: national citizen groups not only privilege experience and expertise (and fail to privilege those who are willing to stay at meetings till the last person leaves). They are increasingly effective in our complex society.

For example, Jeffrey Berry of the Brookings Institution has found that, even though citizen groups constitute fewer than 10 percent of all policy-making and policy-influencing groups in Washington, they constitute a remarkable 32 percent of all groups testifying before Congress—up from 26 percent in the 1970s. And no other kind of group testifies more: trade associations constitute 26 percent of all groups testifying; corporations, 19 percent.

Berry has also discovered that citizen groups are now 46 percent of all interest groups mentioned in television coverage of policy issues. By contrast, corporations are 24 percent and trade associations, 13 percent.

Finally, Berry has found that citizen group research is 19 percent of all research featured in major newspapers—second only to government research at 31 percent. Academic research is 18 percent, and corporate research, 9 percent.

That's clout.

And it's not necessarily left- or right-wing clout. From the outside, citizen groups may seem extremely partisan. But when you wade in, you'll find that most citizen groups are caught up in fascinating dialogues, now, between their radical middle members and their more conventionally partisan members.

For example, if you'd have attended the 2000 annual conference of the left-leaning Children's Defense Fund, you'd have heard many speakers come across in a radical middle key. Susan Schechter, social work professor from the University of Iowa, didn't blame youth violence on unemployment. She blamed it largely on bad parenting. Educator Ted Sizer called for a nationwide commitment to character education in the schools, and conflict resolution expert Linda Lantieri called on schools "to teach young people how to habitually respond in situations of conflict and violence."

A recent National Taxpayers Union conference featured the usual contingent of right-wing tax resenters and tax resisters. But it also featured tax reformers like Alvin Rabushka of the Hoover Institution, who argued that a flat tax could benefit the poor, and Ken Blackwell, Ohio's first African-American Secretary of State, who urged delegates to observe "the duties at our doorstep" (a line from Dickens's *Bleak House*) and fight for "simple and fair" tax reforms at the state and local levels.

A recent NAACP national convention played the usual racial blame games. But it also featured a series of "Youth Program" events that turned into a virtual counter-convention. One young person spoke with great passion about how it feels being told you're "acting white" when you do well in school. Those who voice these insults, he declared, are "just as dangerous" today as those who opposed the civil rights movement in the Sixties.

Even Rotary and Kiwanis are responding to radical middle energies. The "Declaration of Rotarians in Businesses and Professions" includes a pledge to be "fair to my employer, employees, associates, competitors, customers, the public." And at Kiwanis's 88th annual convention in Indianapolis in 2003, delegates reaffirmed their commitment to eliminating iodine deficiency disorder—the world's leading preventable cause of mental retardation—in every country on Earth.

So don't do what I did in the Reagan era and go off and start your own national political group. And don't listen to doubters like Benjamin Barber and Theda Skocpol. Join a national citizen group and find the radical middle energy in it. Then connect with that and make it stronger.

RESOURCES

Texts

For a great and genuinely radical middle primer on community organizing, stressing collaborative problem-solving rather than government- or business-bashing, see Charles Dobson, *The Troublemaker's Teaparty: A Manual for Effective Citizen Action* (2003), partially available with other material at www.vcn.bc.ca/citizens-handbook. For a description of radical-middle-type community organizations, see Carmen Sirianni and Lewis Friedland, *Civic Innovation in America* (2001). For a pioneering look at the positive and negative aspects of small group decision-making, see Jane Mansbridge, *Beyond Adversary Democracy* (1980).

For radical middle aspects of professional associations, just scroll carefully through any major association's website, such as that of the American Political Science Association (www.apsanet.org). For a radical middle analysis of national citizen organizations, see Jeffrey Berry, *The New Liberalism: The Rising Power of Citizen Groups* (1999). For a comparably astute analysis of international nongovernmental organizations like Doctors Without Borders and Refugees International, see Ann Florini, ed., *The Third Force: The Rise of Transnational Civil Society* (2000).

Groups

Radical middle groups that serve community organizations include National Association for Community Mediation (www.nafcm.org), National Civic League (www.ncl.org), Neighborhoods USA (www.nusa.org), and Public Conversations Project (www.publicconversations.org). The Enabling Meaningful Relationships Project of the Institute for Alternative Futures (www.altfutures.com) works with professional associations as well as with community and national groups.

18

DO SOME POLITICAL
SPADEWORK. THEN RUN
FOR OFFICE AND WIN

WHEN MY FRIEND ANN ran for office as a Green Party candidate, she didn't do any polling. She feels pollsters and other professional campaign consultants corrupt the political process. Instead, she created campaign literature that reflected the wants and needs of people as she imagined them to be: "Tax bads, not goods!"; "Build local exchange networks"; "Value our local artists." Although she's a naturally gregarious person, she didn't bother raising much money—in her mind, fundraising is an unseemly task that smacks of the worst of capitalism, and reminds you of your father; and besides, she wants all campaigns to be publicly funded. As a result, she ran no radio or TV ads, even though ads were phenomenally inexpensive in her economically depressed district. And of course she did no political telemarketing.

Ann was running against a laughably underqualified Republican and a little-known Democrat. Her family had deep roots in the district and was well known and well respected. At some point she realized she had a chance to win, and gave about $1,000 to a friend who promised to act as her campaign manager even though her friend had had no genuine campaign experience. Neither Ann nor her friend read any of the many wonderful how-to-run-a-campaign books on the market. After all, those books would have conveyed how things are done in the mainstream, and the last thing Ann wanted to do was reproduce The System. Besides, Ann's friend ended up having personal problems and wasn't able to help much. Ann never asked for her money back. That might have been unkind.

When Ann ended up with 4 percent of the vote, she thought of it as a great victory, by The People, over insurmountable odds.

Ann is a rebel, and it's important to make time for the rebels in your life. Rebellion also makes for great literature—I carried Albert Camus's *The Rebel* around with me for a whole year once. (At the age of 18.) But rebellion is not for the radical middle. If anything underlies our Four Key Values, it's the urge to be of use—to self and others. And when your actions are purer than pure, as Ann's were, that doesn't help anyone. After the humiliating election defeat, you're embittered (despite your brave words), your supporters are demoralized, and everyone else is left scratching their heads or—at best—appreciative of the entertainment you provided.

There is no reason radical middle–oriented men and women can't win electoral office, in any political party. Our politics is both more relevant and more compelling than anything offered by the left or right today. To pave the way, two tasks await us. We need to open up the political process, and we need to learn how to credibly compete for political office.

HELP OPEN UP THE POLITICAL PROCESS

The McCain-Feingold campaign finance reform bill is a paper tiger, and behind the saccharine rhetoric everyone knows it. Under McCain-Feingold, the national political parties aren't supposed to solicit or spend soft money. But state political parties can continue to accept some unlimited donations. And independent political groups and nonprofit organizations—including those whose "independence" is more legal than real—can also continue to raise and spend soft money. As this book goes to press, billionaire George Soros is putting together a $15 million war chest to prevent President Bush from winning a second term. I guarantee, Soros will find ways to spend that money.

Because money will always be sloshing around in political campaigns, public funding of elections would be a disaster. Taxpayers would pour millions of dollars into campaign coffers . . . but many, many more millions of dollars in private funds would show up anyway, through traditional and designer nonprofit organizations and so-called Section 527s, to pay for issue ads and other gimmicks that everyone would know were in support of certain candidates or in opposition to others.

At the radical middle, you don't want to be like Ann and pursue sainthood. You want to make the real world a better place. So radical middle activists don't aspire to stop money's inexorable flow, but open up the political process despite the presence of big money.

To that end, we've proposed five key reforms. What they have in common is they rely more on radical middle cleverness-and-imagination than they do on big government censoring-and-policing:

- **Free media.** Some groups would have media outlets provide free TV and radio time to all candidates who managed to gather a certain number of signatures, or collect a certain number of $5 contributions, or raise a certain amount of money. Free media time would let voters hear from all credible candidates, and in some scenarios would put underfunded challengers on the same footing as incumbents. If the free time came in segments of 15 minutes or more, it would improve political dialogue, too, since glib sound bites wouldn't suffice.
- **Tax credits.** Some groups would have the IRS provide a $50 tax credit (in effect, a free $50 coupon) to all individuals contributing $50 or more to candidates or parties. That should make people of ordinary means a lot more influential in political campaigns—since if millions of taxpayers regularly took advantage of the credit, politicians would know that a substantial portion of their funding was coming from people of ordinary means (approximately $1.2 billion was spent by Presidential and Congressional candidates on the 2000 election; $50 times 15 million taxpayers is more than half that).
- **Proportional representation.** Some groups would change the ground rules of our elections. That's not as pie-in-the-sky as it seems—the ground rules have varied considerably over the course of our history. In one widely discussed scenario, favored by some but not all at the radical middle, we'd do away with single member districts and switch over to a system of "proportional representation" (PR).

Under our current voting system, voters are divided into one-seat districts and "winner takes all." Under PR, we'd have multi-seat districts and many more parties and viewpoints could be represented.

Let's say ten one-seat districts combine into one ten-seat district. A party that wins 10 percent of the popular vote would win one of the ten seats, a party that wins 30 percent would win three seats, and so on. (Many variants are possible, but that's the basic system.) The result? Third parties would be more likely to win seats, members of racial and ethnic minorities might win more seats, and a greater range of political perspectives would almost surely be represented.

Although no U.S. legislature currently uses PR, it's the dominant voting system in free nations. Of the 42 large democracies with high ratings from Freedom House (a widely respected voice for democracy and freedom around the world), only three—the U.S., Canada, and Mongolia—fail to use PR to elect at least one of their national legislatures.

Unlike some good people, I don't support PR. Because it would encourage candidates to make narrow and often divisive appeals to clearly identifiable fragments of the electorate, I think it would drive Americans apart. And divisiveness is not the radical middle way. Besides, candidates like my friend Ann need to learn how to appeal to ordinary Americans—not be given an opportunity to make an end-run around them.

- **Instant runoffs.** Some groups would replace winner-take-all with "instant runoff voting" (IRV). I much prefer IRV to PR.

    Under IRV, we keep one-seat districts. But in every race with three or more candidates, voters would rank them in order of preference. Whenever a vote fails to produce a clear majority for one candidate, the least popular candidate would be eliminated and the second-choice votes of his or her voters would be given to the remaining candidates; and that process would continue until one candidate achieved a majority.

    IRV could accomplish everything positive that PR could accomplish. Votes for third-party and independent candidates would no longer be "wasted," and more of us might come to the polls.

But IRV trumps PR *and* winner-take-all in one very crucial respect. Under both those systems, candidates have a built-in incentive to take polarized and polarizing—positions on the issues. But under IRV, candidates have a built-in incentive to seek out innovative positions that appeal to everyone's best interests—since they're competing for everyone's second-choice votes. So IRV has the unique capacity to encourage a healing, "radical middle" kind of society and discourage the polarization of winner-take-all and the balkanization of PR.

In 2002, San Francisco voters approved a proposition calling for IRV in local elections; and at least 20 other U.S. jurisdictions are thinking about following suit.

- **Nonpartisan redistricting.** Some activists think that the best way to encourage radical middle politics is to create more competitive voting districts. Truly competitive races held every two to four years might induce candidates to run not by rallying their hard-left or hard-right political bases, but by coming up with clever, healing, radical middle public policy solutions to the issues of the day.

One hundred years ago, many races for the House of Representatives were competitive. Half the seats in the 1890s were won by margins of 10 percent or less. But in the year 2000, only 13 percent of House seats were decided by margins of 10 percent or less. What happened?

A line of Supreme Court cases going back to the 1960s began requiring voting districts to have roughly the same number of people. So instead of redrawing district boundary lines only when population changes caused a state to lose or gain seats, legislators began redrawing district lines after every census—every ten years.

On the surface, that was a good thing. But politicians were quick to use the new rules for their own self-serving ends. The majority party in each state capitol carved out a maximum number of safe seats for itself. Or, when the parties were more or less evenly matched, both parties colluded to carve out safe seats for one another. Thanks to ever-more-sophisticated computer programs, legislatures got better and better at creating "designer districts" with safe seats, and now they absolutely dominate the political landscape.

Tom Hofeller, the Republican National Committee's redistricting director, was only being honest when he told the National Conference of State Legislators, "In the politics of redistricting, politicians get to choose the voters."

What can be done? We can insist that redistricting be carried out not by partisan politicians, but by nonpartisan or bipartisan panels.

A very few states are doing that now—most notably, Iowa and Washington. In Iowa, the state legislature has turned the job of redistricting over to the Legislative Service Bureau, a respected, nonpartisan agency that also drafts bills and does research for Iowa legislators. Under the redistricting rules, the Bureau can't look at previous election results, or any demographic information other than population size. Counties are not to be divided and geographic contiguity is to be maintained.

As a result, for years Iowa has boasted some of the most competitive Congressional races in the nation, and some of our most thoughtful and independent Congresspeople.

The best way to create a polarized society is by sticking with winner-take-all elections. The best way to create a balkanized society is by changing over to a system of proportional representation. The best way to create a radical middle society—where politicians will listen to all people, and people will listen to each other—is by moving to instant runoff voting and nonpartisan redistricting.

RUN FOR OFFICE

Even before we attain a more open political process, I'd like you to consider doing the biggest single thing one can possibly do to bring a radical middle society into being: run for political office. Or help some other caring person run for office.

I know it's fashionable to disparage politicians. And if you don't know any, they probably seem like a strange and rare breed. But most politicians are just like anybody else. And they're not rare at all: at last count, there were over 510,000 popularly elected officials in the U.S. Over a million elections are held in every four-year cycle.

Of course, you'll never win elective office if you run with the mindset of my friend Ann. But caring people shouldn't feel obligated to adopt her alienated stance toward elections. Rep. Bob Filner (D-Calif.) went to Mississippi in the Sixties as a white civil rights worker, and was thrown in jail there for his troubles—for two months—at the age of 19. Sen. Tim Johnson (D-S.D.) was brought up by well-educated parents in small towns in the Midwest in the Fifties and Sixties, and like many other kids with similar backgrounds, was extraordinarily restless and idealistic from an early age.

But both Rep. Filner and Sen. Johnson learned how to play the mainstream political game. And it didn't corrupt them in the least. Last year Radical Middle Newsletter's Congressional scorecard found they were the "most visionary members of Congress"—each of them had supported 70–75 percent of the bills we judged to be radical middle.

Don't start at the top. Start down the street—literally. Although local political parties were once on the decline, most of them have turned around in the last 20 years. Some political scientists claim that, on the whole, they've never been stronger—partly because of soft money and partly because they've figured out how to be of use to the new generation of independent-minded candidates.

If you know a local politician, try to make yourself useful to him or her. But even if you don't know anyone on the local scene, it's not too hard to get your feet wet by getting involved in local party affairs. "The local parties are far from being exclusive clubs," says Indiana University Professor Marjorie Hershey, one of the leading students of U.S. party politics. "The 'front doors' are often open to anyone who cares to walk in."

Whether or not your local party is welcoming, attend city council meetings; attend the meetings of other elected bodies you might like to be part of; become familiar enough with the rhythms of your institutions that they lose whatever mystique they may have in your eyes. If you want to bring innovative radical middle ideas into the political arena, you can't feel awed by the institutions you'll be serving.

At the same time, begin breaking down your lack of familiarity with political campaigns and campaigning. One great way of doing this is to actually get involved in a political campaign—they're always looking for volunteers (and not just leafletters: you can volunteer to organize events, research press coverage, or do whatever else you might be good at).

Another, complementary approach you can take is read some of the wonderful books on the market today about the nuts and bolts of campaigning for office. For local elections I recommend Lawrence Gray's *How to Win a Local Election* (rev. 1999) and Catherine Shaw's *The Campaign Manager* (3rd ed. 2004). For big city, state, and Congressional elections I also recommend Ronald Faucheux's *Running for Office* (2002) and Ronald Faucheux, ed., *Winning Elections* (2003).

One thing these books can do is help you overcome the myth that elections are off-limits to anyone without huge gobs of money. Most elections do not require unfathomable amounts of money. And to the extent that money is required, there are many tried and true techniques for raising it which these books summarize.

Another thing these books can do is help you pose certain questions you'll need to ask of yourself: Why do I want to do this? Do I really want to serve in the capacity I seek? Will I respond well to the work and the challenge it will give me? Is it the right time for me? Can I do this to my family?

After one of my newsletter subscribers ran for—and won—a seat on the Alachua County Board of Commissioners (Gainesville, Fla., and environs), he sent me a letter that included these telling passages:

"It finally occurred to me that *I* could be the next commissioner from my county. With an academic background in city planning, with leadership skills gained from serving on a variety of advisory boards, and with the experiences of starting a farmer's market and teaching adult classes in energy conservation, I felt as qualified as anyone. . . .

"My campaign team was unorthodox—to say the least. My earliest supporter was a retired history professor who offered to serve as treasurer. The local president of Friends of the Earth took charge of literature distribution. A 72-year-old Trinidadian responded to my need for car top signs. . . .

"However, I did not shun the more traditional kinds of expertise. I attended a workshop in Daytona called 'How to Run and Win an Electoral Campaign.' And a former City Commissioner offered to counsel me on a regular basis. At these weekly sessions we developed content, style, and process. His major contribution may have been convincing me to simplify my presentations. My immediate task was not to change the world but to win an election."

Throughout this book I've argued that a new and life-giving political perspective is arising, that of the radical middle. I've described some of the innovative and healing new ideas that radical middle thinkers are proposing. I've described how activists are promoting those ideas. But we live in a representative democracy, and before radical middle ideas can replace traditional left- and right-wing ideas, they're going to have to be carried into the political arena by caring men and women with the moxie to run for office. Could one of those caring people be you?

RESOURCES

Texts

For campaign finance reform laws as a paper tiger, see Thomas Edsall, "New Ways to Harness Soft Money in Works," *Washington Post* (25 August 2002). For free media as a better way to open up the political process, see Paul Taylor and Norman Ornstein, "The Case for Free Air Time," Alliance for Better Campaigns (2002), accessible online. For small tax credits to all campaign contributors, see Zach Polett, "Empower Citizens," *Boston Review* (April-May 1997), accessible online, and Matthew Miller, "Patriot Dollars," chap. 9 in *The Two Percent Solution* (2003).

For an insightful discussion of PR and IRV, see Ted Halstead and Michael Lind, *The Radical Center* (2001), 113–19. For an insightful discussion of redistricting, see Joanne Dann, "Safe but Sorry: The Way We Redistrict Destroys the Middle Ground," *Washington Post* (2 December 2001). If you're considering running for office, besides the four how-to books mentioned in this chapter you might benefit from Daniel Shea and Michael Burton's more reflective account, *Campaign Craft*, rev. ed. (2001).

Groups

Many national organizations support the kinds of policies and efforts advocated here, among them the Alliance for Better Campaigns (www.bettercampaigns.org), Annenberg Public Policy Center (www.appcpenn.org), Campaign Finance Institute (www.cfinst.org), Center for Voting and Democracy (www.fairvote.org), and Project Vote Smart (www.votesmart.org).

ACKNOWLEDGMENTS:
DOWN AT THE PICCADILLY

NOW THAT YOU'VE READ THIS FAR, dear reader, I don't need to tell you this book is the end-point of many years of searching. It all began when I left the alternative culture for law school. No, that's unfair . . . began when I snuck away from home on the Greyhound Bus, at the age of 17, to join a group of demonstrators outside the Piccadilly Cafeteria in Dallas, Texas. I was so nervous I could hardly open my mouth, till a lady came up to me and hugged me (I'd hardly ever been hugged before, by anyone; it was 1964) and pinned an index card to my shirt saying, "FREEDOM now. Integrate the Piccadilly. Dallas needs Freedom."

Dallas may still need "Freedom." But I've been blessed with astonishing comrades-in-arms ever since that day, and this book couldn't exist without them.

Spanning four decades now, my intense and sometimes contentious personal-political-spiritual conversations with John Amodeo, Catherine Cascade, Alanna Hartzok, Art Levine, Corinne McLaughlin, Allen Parker, Belden Paulson, Richard B. Perl, Marc Sarkady, Joe Simonetta, John Steiner, and David Thaler, have stretched me as a person, as a political thinker, and as a man.

Whenever I begin to think I put the radical middle together out of whole cloth, all I have to do is remember that my friends Shelley Alpern at Trillium Asset Management Corp., Sam Daley-Harris at RESULTS, Denise Hamler at Co-op America, John Marks at Search for Common Ground, and Mark Mawrence at Fund for Peace, have actually been practicing at their extraordinary organizations (in three cases, for over 20 years) what I am merely preaching in this book.

Years ago, a wonderful New York book editor, Tobi Sanders, spent an inordinate amount of time urging me to write a book combining my political ideas with at least a dollop of my personal-political experiences. About ten minutes after her last encouraging phone call—from a telephone booth by the side of a road in Bucks County, Pennsylvania—her car was struck head-on by a truck, killing her instantly. Hey, Tobi, here it is, babe. Hope you like it.

My Washington, D.C.-based newsletter, *Radical Middle*, which bears some relation to this book, is not kept afloat by foundations or wealthy patrons—its continued existence is due entirely to the generosity of my subscribers. It astonishes me that at this point over 500 of them have contributed over and beyond their subscription fees toward the newsletter's upkeep (and mine). Although a $1 contribution is just as delightful to me as a larger one, I want to single out, for generosity way beyond the call of duty, George Bullard, Kurt Colburn, Randy Compton, Doris Dannemann, Pat Hagan, Ms. Gene K. Hoffman, Bill Holden, David Mayer, Allen Parker, Elsa Porter, Roger Pritchard, and Dick Whittaker.

One of the great things about going to law school at age 46 is you end up with colleagues half your age. Kurt Colburn, John Farina, Brian Israel, Mark Marmer, Jim Power, and David Yamada all played some significant part in my newsletter, this book, or both.

For reasons I don't understand (but in my New Age period I'd have claimed to understand perfectly), over a period of about four months people from coast to coast began hectoring me to write a book or find an agent or publisher for one. Particularly effective were John and Marjorie Ewbank, Jerry Fletcher, David Langer, John Raatz, Michael Shuman, Mal Warwick, and—truly if not for you, kid—Annie Gottlieb.

The very week I realized I could never do justice to the book while continuing to write my newsletter, Nathan Ross, an 83-year-old retired therapist whom I'd met briefly once after giving a talk in Akron, Ohio, in 1978, called from out of the blue to ask what he called an "idle question." If he gave me a small stipend, would I be willing to take time off to put my political ideas in the form of a book?

For invaluable feedback on a draft outline of this book, we should all be grateful to Lucille Chagnon, Jess Middleton, Betty Mullendore, Stan Perrin, Joe Sanders, Jared Scarborough, Pat Smith, Heidi Souza, and David Thaler.

To make sure I didn't commit too many errors here, I put together a dream team of thinkers and activists and had them go over individual chapters: Clem Bezold (health care), Judge Mark Painter (legal reform), Ted Rockwell (energy), Sandy Wassilie (education), Carl House and friends (race), Alanna Hartzok (welfare), Michael Phillips (tax policy), Professor Lewis Solomon (corporations), Walter Truett Anderson (biotech), Joseph Jones (national service), Professor Nicolaus Tideman (globalization), Professor Saul Mendlovitz (humanitarian intervention), and Jerry Fletcher (responses to terrorism).

In addition, I had my old classmate Kurt Colburn, Esq., go over most of the law-related parts, and futurist Dave Snyder go over most of the futures-relevant parts. And Art Levine, Michael Marien, John McClaughry, and Graham Molitor were ornery enough to read and critique the whole thing.

Nearly all my readers made not only corrections but extensive and memorably sardonic comments and suggestions. The book is better for it, and might have been better still if I'd listened to more of what they had to say.

My literary agent, James Levine, is the stuff of authors' dreams. He fought to find not just a publisher for me, but the right publisher. Although he claims to like my message, there's a better way to confirm his radical middle identity. On the one hand, he's super-competent and super-busy. On the other hand, he's one of the few top agents who invites all comers to submit book proposals to his agency without pre-screening and right over the Internet (www.levinegreenberg.com).

It is fashionable now to disparage big publishers, but Westview Presss could not have been more sensitive to my message, or to me. My editor there, Jill Rothenberg, is the old-fashioned kind, demanding and persistent and thorough. No author could have asked for more. And my whole team there, including Rebecca Marks (production), Trish Goodrich and Greg Houle (publicity), and Sara Bercholz and Cathleen Tetro (marketing), is not just competent, it's a collective work group such as we dreamed of in the Sixties. A collective at Westview-Perseus: another radical middle phenomenon.

For nearly a year now I've been looking forward to using this space to thank Allen, Art, Beryl, Dee, Kurt, Valerie, and most especially you, Elizabeth, for being in my life.

Reader, let me tell you something. The people in these acknowledgments are as different from one another as could be imagined, except for this one thing: if they'd all been about my age, and been raised in north Texas, I'd have probably met them all on that demonstration at the Piccadilly.

And that's no small bond.

INDEX

Accuracy in Media, 12
Ackerman, Bruce, 97, 98
Affirmative action
    college admission factors and,
        87–88
    disadvantaged and, 8, 81–89
    economic class discrimination and,
        83–84, 86
    multicultural approach to, 88, 89
    postethnic approach to, 88–89
    racial based type of, 81, 84–85, 86,
        88
    socioeconomic diversity and, 83–85
Ali, Tariq, 168
Al-Qaeda, 162, 169
Alstott, Anne, 97, 98
Alternative Dispute Resolution
    (ADR) programs, 51, 179
Alternative health care, 36, 37,
    42–43, 178
American Academy of Pediatrics, 41
American Association for the
    Advancement of Science
    (AAAS), 191
American jobs and globalization,
    138–141
American Public Health Association,
    93
American Society of International
    Law, 192
AmeriCorps, 126, 127
Anderson, Sherry, 25
Anderson, Walter Truett, 63
Andrewsullivan.com, 183

Annan, Kofi, 155, 157
Antiglobalization movement
    demonstrations by, 137–138
    issues of, 12, 26–27, 138–147
    views on corporations of, 104, 105,
        106–107, 112
Appiah, Anthony, 192
Arab Human Development Report
    2002 (United Nations/Fergany),
    168
Art Levine Confidential, 183
Atlantic, 184
Atta, Mohammad, 167

Barber, Benjamin, 192, 194
Berry, Jeffrey, 193
Best Alternative Medicine, The
    (Pelletier), 42
Beyer, Peter, 119
Bezold, Clement, 37, 108, 192
Biobased energy, 63
"Biodevastation," 116
Biotechnology
    books criticizing, 116
    food and, 115, 117–120
    genetic engineering examples,
        115, 117–118, 120–121
    health and, 115, 117–118, 119,
        120
    human genetics and, 120–123
    polarized pro-/anti- views on, 12,
        116, 121, 122, 123
    radical middle views on, 12,
        13–14, 115–123

Biotechnology *(continued)*
  regulation and, 119–120, 123, 192
  safety and, 118–119
Biotechnology Industry Organization
  (BIO), 116
"Bipartisan Congressional Retreats,"
  27
"Black Hawk Down" incident, 152
Blackwell, Ken, 194
Blair, Margaret, 113
Boshara, Ray, 96–97, 98
Bourne, Randolph, 127
Brookings Institute, 184
Brown, Mark Malloch, 169–170
Buchanan, Pat, 146
Bush, George W., 12, 146, 163
Business Week, 59

Caldera, Louis, 129, 132
Campaign Manager, The (Shaw), 204
Campaigns. *See* Political campaigns
Canfield, Jack, 25
Caplan, Arthur, 123
Caring person, 11–12, 17, 18
Carlson, Rick, 37
Carnegie Commission on Preventing
  Deadly Conflict, 154
Carnevale, Anthony, 85, 86, 87
Carter, Jimmy, 57–58
Center on Policy Attitudes, 12, 37
Centers for Disease Control and
  Prevention (CDC), 41
Chalk, Steve, 59
Chappell, Thomas, 43
Charlie Rose show, 183–184
Children's Defense Fund, 193–194
Choice maximization
  health care and, 7, 13, 36
  industrial era and, 14–15
  law reform and, 7, 48
  overview of, 7
  See also Knowledge era/workers
Chow, Effie, 43
Christian Science Monitor, 183

Clash of Fundamentalisms, The (Ali),
  168
Class Morality Project, 12
Clinton, Bill, 127
Clinton, Hillary, 38
Collins, James, 108–109
"Combined cycle gas turbine," 61–62
Communitarian Platform, 164
Complex public. *See* Creative
  class/public
Conservation of energy, 60–61
Constitution (U.S.), 22–23
"Consumer-service" jobs, 139
Corporate culture reform
  accountants and, 111–112
  board of directors and, 111
  business schooling and, 178–179
  consultants for, 107–109
  executives and, 110–111
  investors and, 112
  laws for, 109–112
  "learning organization" and,
    107–108
  need for, 105–107
  Sarbanes-Oxley Act and, 104, 110,
    111
  scenario planning and, 108
  tax reforms and, 111, 112
Corporations
  antiglobalist view on, 104, 105,
    106–107, 112
  human potential maximization
    and, 8, 13, 103
  left/right political views on,
    103–104, 112–113
  radical middle views on, 104–105,
    113
  shareholder value maximization
    and, 106–107, 109
Council for Responsible Genetics, 122
Creative class/public
  description of, 13, 16
  expansion of, 18
  See also Knowledge era/workers

Crosby, Brian, 72
Crouch, Stanley, 89

Daley-Harris, Sam, 189 190
Dallaire, Romeo, 154
Danzon, Patricia, 39, 40
Darling-Hammond, Linda, 74
Deal, Terrence, 106
Democratic Leadership Council
    (DLC), 23–24
Dependency, 91
Developing countries
    aid to, 9, 14, 169–170
    globalization and, 142–143
Direct democracy, 193
"Disia," 27
Draft. See National service
Drucker, Peter, 21–22
D'souza, Dinesh, 63
Duhl, Leonard, 37
Dyer, Wayne, 25
Dyson, Esther, 19

Economic class discrimination,
    83–84, 86
    See also Affirmative action
Economist, The, 183
Education
    class size and, 71
    costs and, 70, 77, 78–79
    equalizing school funding, 77
    failures in, 70
    federalizing school funding, 77
    principals and, 78
    professional schooling importance,
        176–180
    "raising standards" and, 71
    reforms for, 77–78
    staying informed, 182–184
    union regulations and, 77–78
Educators
    alternative paths to teaching,
        73–74
    apprenticeships for, 74

career-long development for, 75
    evaluations of, 75
    licensing tests for, 74
    need for great teachers, 8, 13,
        69 73, 75–76
    new teaching culture and, 72–78
    pay of, 76
    reforms for, 73–76
    schooling reforms for, 73
Eisenberg, David, 178
Elected offices
    running for, 202–205
    See also Political campaigns
Emotional Intelligence (Goleman),
    109
Employer subsidies and jobs, 93–94
Energy
    biobased energy, 63
    conservation of, 60–61
    costs and, 64–65
    externalities and, 64
    fossil fuels and, 61–62
    hydrogen power, 58, 59, 62
    nuclear energy, 62–63
    oil dependency and, 57–65, 169
    parallel paths for, 7, 58–64
    renewable energy, 61
    values-change path of, 63–64
Enron scandal, 104, 106, 110, 181
Environmental Protection Agency
    (EPA), 119, 120
Environmental standards and
    globalization, 143–145
Erikson, Erik H., 8
Essential Profession, The, 71–72
Estes, Ralph, 113
Etzioni, Amitai, 128, 132
European Union, 142

Fair start
    overview, 7–8
    teachers and, 8, 13, 69–79
Farrell, Warren, 19
Faucheux, Ronald, 204

Federalist Papers, 22–23
Fergany, Nader, 168
Filner, Bob, 203
Florida, Richard, 16
Food and Drug Administration,
    119–120
Fordham Foundation, 74
Foreign aid
    reform goals and, 168–169
    terrorism and, 169
Fossil fuels, 57–65, 61–62, 169
Four Key Values
    caring person and, 12
    knowledge-era norms and, 16
    overview, 6–10
    summary, 6–7
Francois, Joseph, 142–143
Franklin, Benjamin, 22, 58
Freedom House, 200
Freedom-security balance, 162,
    163–165, 167
Freeman, Richard, 24
Free trade
    radical middle and, 9, 12, 14
    views on, 12, 14
Free trade agreements, 141–142
Fukuda-Parr, Sakiko, 119
Fund for Peace, 151
Future Survey, 184

Gardner, Howard, 8, 180, 181
Garten, Jeffrey, 110
Geller, Howard, 60
Generation X, 25–26
Generation Y, 25–26
Gene therapy, 120
Genetic counseling, 121–122
Genetic enhancement, 120, 122
Genetic testing, 120
Gerber, Robin, 128
Germline therapy, 121
Gerzon, Mark, 27
Glastris, Paul, 128
Glendon, Mary Ann, 47

Global Environmental Organization
    (GEO), 144–145
Globalization
    American consumer and, 141–142
    American jobs and, 138–141
    American sovereignty and,
        145–146
    developing countries and,
        142–143
    environmental standards and,
        143–145
    global poverty and, 142–143
    labor standards and, 143–145
    political views overview on,
        146–147
    terrorism and, 171
    See also Antiglobalization
        movement
Golden Rice, 115, 119
Goleman, Daniel, 109
Good Work (Gardner), 180
Gordon, James, 37
Gore, Al, 12
Gottlieb, Annie, 25
Gourevitch, Philip, 154
Gray, Lawrence, 204
Greenbaum, Alex, 141
Gresser, Ed, 139
Groups
    characteristics of radical middle
        groups, 189–190
    local groups, 188–190
    national citizen groups, 192–194
    professional associations, 190–192
Guardian, 183
Gurian-Sherman, Doug, 118, 119

Haass, Richard, 168–169
Habicht, Hank, 59
Hackworth, David, 128
Halstead, Ted, 38
Hamilton, Alexander, 22–23
Harriet Tubman Memorial Hostel
    (The Last Resort), 125

Harrison, Lawrence, 24
Harvey, Philip, 93
Haveman, Robert, 93, 94
Hayden, Tom, 175–176
Health care
  alternative care, 36, 37, 42, 178
  basic benefits package of, 39–40
  choice maximization and, 7, 13, 36
  Congress response to, 35–36
  costs of, 40, 41, 45
  crisis of, 35
  employer-based system of, 38
  insurance for, 38–39
  integrative care, 42–43
  medical schooling and, 178
  preventive care, 37, 40–41
  private health care, 37–40
  public health and, 43–45
  radical middle summary views on,
    36–37
  senior prescription drugs and,
    35–36
  single-payer system of, 36
  subsidy for, 39
  universality of, 37–40
Heritage Foundation, 152
Hershey, Marjorie, 203
Hess, Frederick, 74
Hoffman, Stanley, 167
Hollinger, David, 89
Hollings, Fritz, 129
Houghton, Amo, 153
Houston, Jean, 25
How to Win an Election (Gray), 204
Hoyer, Steny, 153–154, 155
Human cloning, 13–14
Human potential maximization
  biotechnology and, 13–14, 116
  corporations and, 8, 13, 103
  national service and, 131–132
Hydrogen fuel cell, 62
Hydrogen power, 58, 59, 62

Ignatieff, Michael, 154

Independent, 183
Individual Development Accounts
    (IDAs), 95–96
Industrial era, 14–16
Information sources, 183–184
Ingraham, Laura, 163
Instant runoff voting, 200–201
Integrative health care, 42–43
International Labor Organization
    (ILO), 144–145
Internet resources, 183, 184
Intervention (military)
  "culture of death" and, 154
  how to intervene, 157–158
  left/right political views on,
    151–152
  New Peace Movement and,
    150–152
  reasons for, 9, 152–154
  right to intervene, 155–156
  Rwanda and, 154, 155, 157
  U.N. and, 152–153, 154, 155–156,
    157–158
  when to intervene, 156–157
In These Times, 183
Iraq war, 149
Israel-Palestine issue, 162, 167–168,
    170
Ivins, Molly, 163

James, William, 127
Jay, John, 22–23
Jefferson, Thomas, 22
Jobs
  American jobs and globalization,
    138–141
  dependency and, 91–92
  employer subsidies and, 93–94
  preparation for, 94–98
  public-sector jobs, 92–93
  social change in workplace,
    180–182
  stakeholder accounts and, 94–98
  work importance, 92

Jobs for All Coalition, 24
Johnson, Tim, 203
Judicial Arbitration and Mediation
    Services, 51

Kahlenberg, Richard, 24, 85, 87
Kaus, Mickey, 128, 132
Kelley, Marjorie, 108
Kendall, David, 37
Kennedy, Allan, 106, 110
Kennedy, Robert F., 23
King, Martin Luther, Jr., 23
Kitcher, Philip, 122
Kiwanis, 194
Klein, Naomi, 27, 105
Knowledge era/workers
    description of, 15–16, 16
    norms of, 16–17, 21–22
    See also Creative class/public
Kohut, Andrew, 12
Korten, David, 27, 104, 105,
    106–107
Kramer, Rita, 73
Kucinich, Dennis, 25
Kull, Steven, 12
Kuttner, Robert, 96, 98

Labor standards and globalization,
    143–145
Landes, David, 105
Lantieri, Linda, 194
Law reform
    choice maximization and, 7, 48
    intimidation and, 49
    law school and, 179–180
    mediation and, 50–51
    problem-solving courts, 51–54
    in processes/practices, 47–55
    restorative justice, 54
    small claims courts and, 49–50
    "therapeutic jurisprudence,"
        54–55
Lay, Ken, 106, 110
"Learning organizations," 107–108

Legal system. See Law reform
Lerner, Michael, 25
Lévy, Bernard-Henri, 168–169
Liberia and U.N. intervention, 153
Licensing tests (educators), 74
Lind, Michael, 128
Litigation Explosion, The (Olson), 48
Los Angeles Times, 85, 183
Lovins, Amory, 116
Lurquin, Paul, 117

Madison, James, 22–23
Magazine resources, 183, 184
Mander, Jerry, 145
Manual for Draft-Age Immigrants to
    Canada (Satin), 28, 125
Mansbridge, Jane, 195
Marien, Michael, 184
Marx, Karl, 105
McCain-Feingold campaign finance
    reform bill, 198
McCloskey, Pete, 127
McCurdy, David, 127
McGovern, Jim, 153
McNamara, Robert, 127
Mead, Lawrence, 24
Mead, Margaret, 127
Mediation, 50–51, 179
Mendlovitz, Saul, 158
Meyerson, Debra, 180, 181
Midtown Community Court,
    Manhattan, 52–53
Mitchell, Lawrence, 110
Molitor, Graham, 192
Moore, Michael, 27, 163
Moskos, Charles, 127, 128
Multicultural approach (affirmative
    action), 88, 89
Murray, Charles, 24
Muslims, 163, 167, 168–169

NAACP, 194
Nader, Ralph, 48
NAFTA, 142

Nathan, Joe, 77
National Academy of Sciences
  (NAS), 118, 119
National Association of Elementary
  School Principals, 78
National Association of Secondary
  School Principals, 78
National Association of Social
  Workers, 93
National Board for Professional
  Teaching Standards, 75, 76
National Center for Complementary
  and Alternative Medicine
  (NCCAM), 42
National Council of Churches
  (NCC), 63
National Endowment for
  Democracy, 24
National Jobs for All Coalition, 93
National Organization for Women,
  12
National sales tax, 97
National service
  benefits of, 131–132
  community service tasks overview,
    130–131
  compensation for, 129–130
  cost/benefit analysis of, 132–133
  duty to country and, 126–128
  for everyone, 129
  homeland security tasks overview,
    130
  left/right political views and, 128
  military tasks overview, 130
  options for, 9, 126, 127, 128, 129,
    130–131
  plans for, 128–131
  support for, 128
  training for, 129
Nation, The, 152, 183
Natural gas, 61–62
"Negative income tax
    experiment"/"SIME-DIME,"
    92

Neoconservatives, 24
Neoliberals, 23–24
Neopopulists, 24
*New Age Politics: Healing Self and
    Society* (Satin), 28–29, 187
New American Foundation, 38, 89,
    96, 141, 184
New Options newsletter, 29
New Republic, The, 183
Newspaper resources, 183
Newsweek, 85
New World Alliance, 29, 187–188
New York Times, 183
New York Times Book Review, 183
No Contest (Nader), 48
Nonpartisan redistricting, 201–202
Non-renewable resources tax, 97–98
Nuclear energy, 62–63
Nunn, Sam, 127

Observer, 183
Office of Disease Prevention and
    Health Promotion, 44
O'Hanlon, Michael, 158
Oil dependency, 57–65, 169
Olson, Walter, 48
Open Society Institute, 181
O'Reilly, Bill, 163
Organizations. *See* Groups; *specific
    organizations*
Ornish, Dean, 25, 43
Oxfam International, 138, 140

Painter, Mark, 50
Palestine-Israel issue, 162, 167–168,
    170
Partnership for Prevention, 44
Patriot Act, 164–165
Pauly, Mark, 39, 40
Peace movements
  for today, 150–152
  Vietnam war era and, 125–126,
    133, 149–150, 151, 191
  See also Intervention (military)

Peck, Scott, 25
Pelletier, Kenneth, 42, 43
Perle, Richard, 24
Peters, Charlie, 23
Pew Research Center, 12, 153,
    166–167
Phelps, Edmund, 93–94
Poarch, Maria, 12
Political campaigns
    free media for, 199
    funding for, 197, 198–199
    instant runoff voting and, 200–201
    McCain-Feingold campaign
        finance reform bill, 198
    nonpartisan redistricting and,
        201–202
    proportional representation and,
        199–200
    rebels and, 197–198
    reforms for, 199–202
    running for office, 202–205
    tax credits and, 199
Postethnic approach (affirmative
    action), 88–89
Potrykus, Ingo, 119
Poverty
    globalization and, 142–143
    UNDP plan and, 169–170
Prenatal testing, 120, 121–122
Prescription drugs for seniors,
    35–36
Preventive health care, 37, 40–41
Problem-solving courts, 51–54
"Producer-service" jobs, 139
"Production tax credit" (PTC), 61
Professional schooling importance,
    176–180
Program on Corporations, Law &
    Democracy (POCLAD), 104
Program on International Policy
    Attitudes, 153
Progressive Policy Institute, 139, 184
Proportional representation,
    199–200

Public Agenda Online, 12
Public Agenda polling firm, 71, 73
Public Citizen, 143–144
Public Conversations Project, 189
Public health, 43–45
Public-sector jobs, 92–93

Rabushka, Alvin, 194
"Radiation imaging" technology, 166
Radical Middle, 184
Radical middle
    early beginnings of, 22–23
    emergence of, 3, 11, 12
    examples of, 3–5
    Four Key Values of, 6–7
    as majority, 12–14
    overview, 5–6
    political forces contributing to,
        23–26
    professional schooling and,
        176–180
    social change in workplace,
        180–182
    staying informed, 182–184
Radical Middle newsletter, 30
Rangel, Charles, 129
Ray, Paul, 25
Real, Terrence, 25
Reason, 183
Redistricting, 201–202
Reich, Robert, 63
Reiss, Michael, 122
Renewable energy, 61
Restorative justice, 54
RESULTS, 99, 181, 189–190
Rewarding Work (Phelps), 93–94
Rifkin, Jeremy, 58, 116, 122
Rodriguez, Gregory, 89
Rose, Stephen, 85, 86, 87
Rotary, 194
Rowley, Coleen, 181
Running for office, 202–205
Running for Office (Faucheux), 204
Rustin, Bayard, 119

Rwanda, 154, 155, 157

Saletan, William, 116
Sarbanes-Oxley Act, 104, 110, 111
Sarkady, Marc, 167
Scenario planning, 108
Schechter, Susan, 194
Schwartz, Peter, 108
Search for Common Ground, 151,
    168
Security-freedom balance, 162,
    163–165, 167
"Self-aggrandizing individual," 17
"Self-sacrificing individual," 17–18,
    193
Senge, Peter, 107–108
Senior prescription drugs, 35–36
Shacochis, Bob, 152
Shareholder value maximization,
    106–107, 109
Shaw, Catherine, 204
Shehadeh, Raja 168
Sherraden, Michael, 95, 96
Shostak, Arthur, 16–17
Silver, Lee, 117
"SIME-DIME"/"negative income tax
    experiment," 92
Sizer, Ted, 194
Skilling, Jeff, 110
Skocpol, Theda, 192, 194
Slate.com, 183
Small claims courts, 49–50
"Smart ID cards," 166–167
Snyder, David, 139
Social change in workplace, 180–182
Somalia and U.N. intervention,
    152–153
Soros, George, 198
Stakeholder accounts and jobs,
    94–98
Stock, Gregory, 117, 122
Strangers in the House: Coming of
    Age in Occupied Palestine
    (Raja), 168

Straughan, Roger, 122
Street Law, Inc., 49
Student Nonviolent Coordinating
    Committee, 28, 91, 176
Students for a Democratic Society
    (SDS), 21, 176
Summit, Pat, 19
Supreme Court
    race-based affirmative action and,
        84
    redistricting and, 201
Surveillance technology, 165–167
Sweeney, John, 138

Tariffs. See Trade restrictions
Tax on non-renewable resources,
    97–98
Teachers. See Education; Educators
Tellus Institute, 64
Temes, Peter, 72, 75
Tempered Radicals (Meyerson),
    180
Terrorism
    being tough on, 162, 163–167
    being tough on causes of, 162,
        167–170
    costs and, 169–170
    economic development and, 9, 14
    freedom-security balance and,
        162, 163–165, 167
    globalization and, 171
    opportunities from, 170–171
    overview, 161–163
    Patriot Act and, 164–165
    surveillance technology and,
        165–167
"Therapeutic jurisprudence," 54–55
Tideman, Nicolaus, 97–98
Tikkun, 25
Toronto Anti-Draft Programme, 28,
    125
Trade restrictions
    as a tax, 141
    global poverty and, 142–143

Trade restrictions *(continued)*
   Muslim exports and, 169
   steel tariff (U.S./2002), 146
Transformationalists, 25
*Travels in the Genetically Modified
   Zone* (Winston), 118
Turner, Grace-Marie, 37

Unger, Roberto, 24
United Nations
   Arab Human Development
      Report 2002, 168
   Charter of, 155–156, 157
   Development Program, 117,
      169–170
   genocide and, 156
   human poverty and, 169–170
   Liberia intervention by, 153
   military intervention and,
      152–153, 154, 155–156,
      157–158
   Security Council of, 155, 157
   Somalia intervention by,
      152–153
Uruguay Round, 142
Ury, William, 104
U.S. Department of Health,
   Education, and Welfare, 92
U.S. Preventive Services Task Force
   (USPSTF), 40
U.S. Public Health Service, 45
Utne Reader, 25

Vietnam war/era
   national service and, 125–126,
      128, 133
   peace movements, 125–126, 133,
      149–150, 151, 191
VISTA, 127
Voting. *See* Political campaigns

Waldman, Steven, 132
Walsch, Neale Donald, 25
Washington, George, 22
Washington Monthly, 23, 184
Washington Post, 183
Watkins, Sherron, 181
"Wealth tax," 97
Weber, Max, 105
Weekly Standard, The, 183
Weil, Andrew, 42
West, Cornel, 24
"What Would Jesus Drive?"
   campaign, 63
White House Commission on
   Complementary and
   Alternative Medicine Policy,
   42–43
*Whose Trade Organization?:
   Corporate Globalization and
   the Erosion of Democracy*
   (Public Citizen), 143–144
Williamson, Marianne, 25
Williams, Patricia, 116
Winning Elections (Faucheux), 204
Winston, Mark, 117, 118–119, 120
Wired magazine, 58
Wolfe, Alan, 12, 13
Woodrow Wilson Center, 153
World Bank, 142
World Future Society, 192
World Trade Center attack (1993),
   163
World Trade Organization (WTO),
   142, 143, 145–146
Wuthnow, Robert, 188

Yankelovich, Daniel, 12, 71
Yousef, Ramzi, 163

Zoellick, Robert, 142